Racing With
"The Doctor"

Todd R. Thomas

The conversations in this book all come from the author's recollections, though they are not written to represent word-for-word transcripts. Rather, the author has retold them in a way that evokes the feeling and meaning of what was said, based on his memories, and the essence of the dialogue is accurate to the best of his abilities.

ISBN-10: 1985070456
ISBN-13: 978-1985070455

To Logan and Hannah, so you know what your dad was doing
all those summer Saturday nights.

God speed Jerry, we sure had a lot of fun.
I'll see you again one day.

Jerry Crabb won the Masters Classic feature at the Knoxville Raceway last Saturday night. Crabb is pictured above with second place finisher John Bankston (far right) and Billy Engelhart in third. Presenting the trophy for the night was Kathy Visser.

L-R: Billy Engelhart, Jerry Crabb, Kathy Visser, and John Bankston.
Dirt Digest, June 5, 1998, issue. (Mike Roberts photo)

Cover Photo: L-R, Jerry Crabb leaning over left rear tire, Todd
Thomas sitting on right rear tire, Tracie Wilson kneeling, Jan Crabb
standing. (author's collection)

CONTENTS

Acknowledgments

Thanks to my brother-in-law, for the introduction to sprint car racing, John, for keeping me included, Twedt, for letting me hang around, and Jerry, for the opportunity to be a part of something I loved. Also, thanks to my cousin for the encouragement and advice, and for listening to my ramblings about racing.

Thanks goes to Bill Wright, for permission to use photos from the National Sprint Car Hall of Fame & Museum collection, and to Dave Hill, for help in tracking down photographers.

Special thanks to knoxvilleraceway.com and woosprint.com for their history sections. The treasure trove of information found therein is invaluable. Also, thanks to the National Sprint Car Hall of Fame & Museum for the ability to purchase Knoxville Raceway Weekly DVD's going back to 1993, which allowed me to relive the events that occurred on the night of May 30, 1998.

The Man in the Arena

It is not the critic who counts;
not the man who points out how the strong man stumbles,
or where the doer of deeds could have done them better.
The credit belongs to the man who is actually in the arena,
whose face is marred by dust and sweat and blood;
who strives valiantly; who errs,
who comes short again and again,
because there is no effort without error and shortcoming;
but who does actually strive to do the deeds;
who knows great enthusiasms,
the great devotions;
who spends himself in a worthy cause;
who at the best knows in the end the triumph of high
achievement,
and who at the worst,
if he fails,
at least fails while daring greatly,
so that his place shall never be with those cold and timid souls
who neither know victory nor defeat.

Theodore Roosevelt

Excerpt from the speech "Citizenship in a Republic," delivered
at the Sorbonne, in Paris, France, on April 23, 1910.

Whatever it Takes

Jerry Crabb leaned forward in the cockpit of his sprint car, and sported an all too familiar scowl on his face. The fifty-something-year-old's right hand rested on the top bar at the front of the roll cage, and his index finger tapped impatiently. "Come on Nelson, let's go!" he barked over his shoulder.

Ron Nelson, Jerry's longtime friend and crewmember, sat in the driver's seat of Jerry's Dodge van parked directly behind the sprint car in the driveway of Jerry's shop. He muttered something unintelligible, likely profane, under his breath, and then slowly nudged the sprint car with the van onto SW 9th, one of the busier four-lane streets on the south side of Des Moines.

Disrupting traffic from both directions Jerry pointed his sprint car north, down the hill just north of Lincoln High School, through a gritty tree-lined neighborhood consisting of small businesses and private residences. His attempts to merge with the normal vehicles traveling the street could not quite be described as courteous.

For those unfamiliar, a sprint car is anything but street-legal. A spartan vehicle, it consists of four open wheels connected to two solid axles, which are attached to a tubular chromoly frame. An eight-cylinder fuel injected open header small block Chevy resides directly in front of the driver, who sits bolt upright surrounded by a roll cage. A tear drop fuel tank is located at the rear.

A small wing is mounted at the front of the car and a large wing sits atop the cage. The wings create downforce to improve traction while speeding around dirt tracks. However for the purpose at hand the top wing sat in the shop, as it wasn't necessary and kind of in the way while the car rolled down the city street.

A sprint car contains no headlights, turn signals, windshield, or glass of any type. No rearview or sideview mirrors, and no exhaust system that would conform to any sort of city noise ordinance. And certainly no glove box to hold registration or insurance information, and no license plate, for that matter.

There is no speedometer in the dashboard, although there is a tachometer, and gauges for oil pressure and water temperature. Not lacking is safety equipment, which far exceeds that of a passenger or commercial vehicle. It's probable that traffic fatalities would become nearly nonexistent if street vehicles utilized the roll cage, seat, and safety harness of a sprint car. However the decrease in comfort and increase in cost would likely make doing that unrealistic.

Lightweight and extremely over-horsepowered, these vehicles are all race car and have no business travelling city streets.

It was interesting to observe the reactions of the passenger and commercial vehicle drivers when they encountered a sprint car sharing their roadway. Some were clearly startled and tended to hang back, I assume to avoid any contact with this odd-looking vehicle that had invaded the routine of their day. Or they appeared curious, yet kept a safe distance to view just exactly what this crazy person driving this buggy-looking machine might do next. Others simply ignored the contraption and continued on their way, obliviously passing by Jerry on the way to wherever they were going. Sometimes they even switched lanes and positioned their cars in between the coasting sprint car and the van that followed it down the hill. Others appeared annoyed, and on more than one occasion gave Jerry the middle finger salute. In any case it gave these drivers a story to tell later in the day.

Fortunately this coast down the hill only lasted a couple of blocks and Jerry made a left turn into the parking lot of a small accounting firm. This was sometimes a tricky maneuver depending on the amount of oncoming traffic headed south. It was a timing thing. He preferred to coast the car onto the parking lot unimpeded rather than stopping for traffic to pass by, which would require an additional push from the van to reach the parking lot. I know he preferred to handle it this way because I've witnessed him having close calls in front of, amongst, and immediately behind oncoming traffic in his attempts to make the turn.

As he coasted onto the level parking lot and the effect of gravity slowed his momentum, Jerry steered as far left as possible in order to point the sprint car back south in the direction of his shop. If he didn't get a good enough run off the street this little procedure sometimes took some manual effort. This is where I came in.

Nelson pulled the van onto the parking lot and I jumped out of the passenger door as we rolled to a stop. The turning radius of a sprint car is not near as sharp to the left as it is to the right, so sometimes it is a chore to maneuver a stationary one towards the intended direction.

While sprint cars circle dirt tracks in a counter-clockwise direction, obviously turning to the left, they spend much of their time turning right while sliding through corners. Think back to Driver's Ed and how they told you to steer into a skid, and that's basically how sprint cars travel through corners. If set up correctly it doesn't take much of a turn to the left to start the slide into a corner, so by design there isn't much concern to steer sharply in that direction.

I asked then future Knoxville Raceway Hall of Fame driver Mike Twedt about this several years ago while helping him push his sprint car. Someone pointed out that a sharp left turn would appear to cause the left front tire to rub the steering link, which travels along the left side of the car. He simply stated that if a driver needs to turn that sharply to the left while racing, he had more immediate concerns to contend with.

So I pushed forward while Jerry turned left and pushed backwards while he turned right a few times until the car was pointed in the right direction. If you have ever tried to jockey around your passenger car 180 degrees in a tight spot, you get the idea. I enjoyed the added bonus of listening to Jerry growl that I was not moving fast enough.

Nelson pulled the van in behind the sprint car and pushed it back onto the street headed south, once again disrupting traffic. Jerry stopped on the road and worked the gear slider handle to place the car in gear. Since a sprint car does not have a self-starting system or transmission, to start one it needs to be put in gear and then push started with another vehicle, hence the van.

A sprint car is always either in gear or out of gear. To confirm it is in gear it is normal practice to rock the car back and forth and feel the resistance if it is properly in gear. Again, this is where I came in.

As I did this rocking, still enjoying Jerry's comments that I was still not moving fast enough, I had my left hand grasped to the sprint car's rear push bumper. Unfortunately, Nelson did not see this and pulled the van up and made my ring finger a sandwich between the push bumper at the front of the van and the rear bumper of the sprint car. I was married at the time and luckily wore my wedding ring, as the band gave my finger some protection. I said a bad word and hopped back in the van.

Jerry waved that he was ready and Nelson put his foot to the gas pedal of the van, pushing the sprint car back up the hill. Jerry opened the fuel valve, waited for oil pressure to build, pumped the throttle a couple of times, and flipped the magneto switch to the "on" position.

With a sight and sound that I will never grow tired of, the sprint car's engine belched, bellowed, and erupted to life. If you ever hear a fuel injected open header sprint car engine start up you will not soon forget the experience. It is similar to the sound of a Harley starting, only louder and more intense. The sound is very crisp. If you are standing next to one of these machines while it is running you can feel the vibration throughout your entire body. I have seen and heard literally thousands of these engines start and it still regularly startles me. I am pretty sure I have suffered some hearing loss because of these engines. I believe it was worth it.

I've sometimes wondered what the drivers in their passenger cars thought if they happened to be alongside Jerry when the engine fired in his sprint car. I think it would have scared the crap out of them. It makes me chuckle to imagine that a soccer mom out running errands may have had to go

4

home and change her underpants after experiencing Jerry's car starting procedure firsthand.

After the sprint car started, Jerry basically left Nelson and me standing still. Yes, he could have simply idled the car back up the hill to his shop. But, after all, he is a race car driver. By the time Nelson pulled the van back onto the shop's parking lot, Jerry was already out of the cockpit and attaching the timing light to the number one spark plug wire while the car sat idling.

As soon as we were within earshot, Nelson and I received orders from Jerry in rapid-fire succession: block a wheel to keep the car from rolling, take the timing cover off, get the magneto lock nut wrench and loosen the nut, and several other things that I don't remember. As per usual Nelson and I ran into and tripped over each other as we tried to meet the demands.

This whole process always made me feel a bit uneasy. I think I worried about what would happen if the local authorities ever observed this activity. Actually it did happen a couple of times, thankfully in my absence.

On one occasion a traffic officer drove by immediately after Jerry turned into his parking lot. She just kept on driving, shaking her head. I imagine she didn't want to wake that sleeping dog.

On another occasion an officer with "Squad Commander" printed on the side of his police car, or something to that effect, pulled into the shop after Jerry completed this procedure. Jerry simply walked up to the police car, grinned, and leaned up against it with his arms crossed. The officer sat in his car, also grinned, and repeatedly said, "I can't f*****g believe it." No warnings or tickets were issued, but the officer did say that if a complaint was registered they would need to do something about it.

For some reason I don't believe anyone ever seriously complained about this practice. Perhaps race fans lived along that street? It likely helped that Jerry would normally wait until rush hour was over, or close to it.

There was a time when one of Jerry's neighbors, who Jerry had never met, stopped by the shop with his small son. He said that on a recent evening, while he sat inside his home, he was startled when he heard Jerry's engine come to life.

The neighbor exclaimed to his wife, "That sounds like a sprint car!" He was right of course, and traced the sound back to Jerry's shop. He simply wanted to show his son a real race car up close.

I never agreed to drive the push vehicle though. In later years, when I no longer had time to spend at Jerry's shop and restricted my racing activities to Saturday nights at Knoxville, and Nelson had moved on to other things, Jerry enlisted the help of his then girlfriend and future wife Jan to drive the van.

Jan, one of the nicest and most caring people I've ever met, but also just as stubborn and outspoken as Jerry, is probably only five foot nothing and would not tip the scales past 100 pounds even if she was soaking wet. Jan driving that full-size Dodge van and pushing Jerry in his sprint car down that busy street, his t-shirt sleeves and unbuckled safety harness belts flapping in the wind, was likely quite a sight.

This process was a regular occurrence outside Jerry's shop on SW 9th during his sprint car racing years. Whenever he did any work that required him to start the engine, this is what he did. There have been products on the market which allows a sprint car team to start the engine while the car is in a stationary position. However the cost of such a luxury item normally far exceeds what the average grassroots racer is willing to spend. For the low-budget team, in a decision whether to purchase such an item versus, say, tires and fuel, tires and fuel wins every time.

I've often heard of other teams starting their cars on quiet city streets, county highways, gravel roads, parking lots, or farm fields. But I've never heard of any starting them on busy, crowded, four-lane main artery city streets – just a couple miles south of downtown Des Moines.

I must admit, the first time I saw Jerry do this I thought he was crazy. Actually, at first I thought he was kidding, then I thought he was crazy. But looking back, that activity really described Jerry in a nutshell.

He did whatever it took to go racing.

End of an Era

In the spring of 2006 I made my annual call to Jerry on the day prior to Knoxville Raceway's practice night. It was Good Friday, I had the day off from work, and figured I better make the call to see what was up for the racing season.

This call seemed to come later and later every year. When I first started helping Jerry with his sprint car I didn't need to make the call because I was in contact with him throughout the off-season. I regularly stopped by his shop to visit or help with preparing the car for the upcoming season. But as the years rolled by and responsibilities grew and time became scarce, I rarely stopped by the shop. A phone call was necessary just to find out what Jerry's racing plans were for the summer, and to see if I was still welcome to help.

Normally these calls were short and to the point, with Jerry saying something like, "Are you on board? Good. See you on opening night." Not much chit-chat with Jerry if he was busy.

This day was different. Thanks to his caller ID he answered the phone saying, "So, what are you up to?"

We caught up on what happened to each other over the winter. He married Jan and they moved into their trailer home, which sat on 40 acres of southern Iowa land they recently purchased, and they were making plans to build a house. He was still working as a television repairman at his shop on SW 9th, but only three days a week. He made the drive to his shop in Des Moines and back those three days, and Jan did the same for her job five days a week. He was looking for a 40 or 50 horsepower tractor to move dirt on his farm. His shop on SW 9th was still up for sale. The man who made an offer for the building was trying to low-ball him, according to Jerry.

He asked how I was doing. I told him about my new job, and how my daughter was 9 going on 19. I explained how my son still loved skateboarding, even after breaking his leg the previous summer, and how he had let his hair grow long - without my approval - but I kept relatively quiet since he's a good kid and earned good grades in school.

Basically we chit-chatted, which was rather unusual. And then came the news that I always knew would someday come.

"I don't know what I'm going to do this year. I haven't touched the car. I'm planning on running Masters, but I don't know beyond that. We're going to go watch the races on the 22nd, but not race. I'll see what I feel like after that," he said.

We talked about the skyrocketing cost of racing, and he told me about another local racer who recently had a 360 cubic inch engine built which pulled over 700 horsepower on the dyno. We guessed how much that cost, and I mentioned that he probably wouldn't want to add up all the money he had spent on racing over the years. He once again stated that he hadn't spent near as much money on his racing operation as most others had on theirs, and I don't believe a truer statement could have been made.

I told him to let me know if he definitely decided to do something for the racing season, and we said our goodbyes. I pressed the phone's off button and laid it on my kitchen table, and reflected for a moment.

For me it was the end of an era.

Origins of a Sprint Car Junkie

I was 18 years old in 1985 when I attended my first sprint car race, which took place at the half-mile Southern Iowa Speedway in Oskaloosa, Iowa. I was fresh out of high school and looking for fun things to do before starting college in the fall.

My brother-in-law had a buddy who raced what was known as a "thunder truck." These vehicles could be described as street stock pickups, and they raced regularly at the Oskaloosa track. One night my brother-in-law asked if I'd like to go watch his buddy race. I said, "Sure, what the heck." Unbeknownst to me, sprint cars happened to be on the card that night too.

Admittedly, I wasn't overly thrilled with that first outing. I don't remember the winner that night, or any of the drivers who raced. Sprint cars were only one of several classes of race cars competing at the track, and there weren't very many of them.

Still, there was something that was very interesting about these strange looking contraptions with the big wing on top, sliding sideways in the corners and slinging rooster tails of clay over the fence. I thought that was pretty cool.

I didn't become hooked until shortly thereafter when I attended my first race at the famed Knoxville Raceway in Knoxville, Iowa, Sprint Car Capital of the World and Home of the Nationals. Why it took me 18 years to drive the 25 miles from my home to visit this world-famous half-mile speed plant is beyond me. Head stuck in the sand, or maybe up a part of my anatomy, would probably explain it best.

I had heard of Knoxville Raceway before. Every Iowan, especially one who lives in Marion County, has heard of Knoxville Raceway. I remember seeing part of a sprint car race, at some other racetrack somewhere, one afternoon on network TV many years ago. I recall hearing the name "Wolfgang" and thought, "Hasn't he raced at Knoxville before?"

Maybe it's the natural modesty Iowans are known for, but I believe most non-race fan residents just don't quite believe Knoxville is that big of a deal. They know there are races there, but not much beyond that. Race fan Iowans, however, know full well about the gem located in the Marion County county seat. But it is somehow overlooked by their non-race fan fellow residents.

I once again went with my brother-in-law, who had attended races previously at Knoxville. We made our way south down Highway 14 and through the rolling hills and farm country of Marion County. After crossing the mile-long bridge over Red Rock Reservoir it only took a few minutes before we reached Knoxville city limits.

We rolled onto the Marion County Fairgrounds and parked right next to the billboard where the National Sprint Car Hall of Fame & Museum now sits off turn two. At that time only barns sat along the backstretch, and the big white fences that lined the perimeter of the track's corners were made of wood. There was no such thing as a luxury suite at a dirt track, and the lighting was pre-Musco. Yet, the outside of the place was impressive.

As we walked to the ticket office I was struck to see how happy and friendly everyone mingling behind the big grandstand seemed to be. Many wore t-shirts with pictures of sprint cars printed on them, along with the names of drivers I didn't recognize. They all had a gleam in their eyes and simply appeared to enjoy being there. I would soon find out the main reason why.

We bought our tickets and walked through the main entrance under the south side of the grandstand. I made note of the excellent product placement of the beer stand just to the left of the entrance, and also noticed a multitude of racing

10

souvenir stands to the left and to the right. Perhaps this was where some of these folks purchased their t-shirts.

We walked straight through and exited on the other side of the grandstand, took a right, and headed for Section B. Once we reached the top step at the bottom row of seats, I turned and faced north, and my first view of the track made my jaw drop.

Even then the place was a first-class facility. The bright white fence contrasted with the black river bottom gumbo dirt track, and colorful billboards lined the inside guardrail of the front straightaway.

The track was wide and had big, sweeping corners. The pits were packed with what seemed to be hundreds of trucks, trailers, and colorful sprint cars, swarmed by guys wearing t-shirts and jeans. They looked as if they had been there for several hours already. The track shined with water and the push trucks were just pulling out to pack the track.

We climbed up past several rows in the grandstand and found our pick of seats, and I sat and became entertained watching the push trucks wheel pack and slip and slide around the track. I then began a barrage of questions directed towards my brother-in-law.

What are those push trucks doing? Why do they circle the track in the opposite direction? What size engines do these cars have? What is a limited sprint (now known as a 360) as compared to a sprint (now known as a 410)? What is the purpose of a heat race? What are B and A features? How fast do they go? And so on, and so forth.

He answered as best he could and said the push trucks were putting the final touches on track preparation, working in the water and manicuring it to create the finest racing surface possible.

He really didn't know why the push trucks circled the track clockwise. (I heard years later a track official said that sometimes they just go in a different direction because they feel like it. It seems there should be more to it than that. I presumed they "worked it in" clockwise because the cars "worked it out" counter-clockwise.)

He explained that the limited sprints had smaller engines (now 360 cubic inch) and smaller top wings and no nose wings (at the time). The sprints had larger engines (now 410 cubic inch), larger top wings, and small wings on the nose.

He described that in each class the heat races were used for drivers to qualify for the A feature, which was the top race of the night. The B feature was used as a last-chance race to qualify for the A feature if the driver didn't advance out of his heat race.

He said they were damn fast. At the time the track record for the sprints was 16.942 seconds, held by Bobby Allen from Hanover, Pennsylvania, which averaged over 106 M.P.H. for the lap. (The current track record as of the end of 2017, set in 2006 by Australian Brooke Tatnell, is 14.407 seconds for an average of nearly 125 M.P.H.)

He eventually gave me the look of, "Why don't you just shut up and watch?"

Around that time the cars were lined up in the staging area of the pits and being pushed off for their turn at wheel packing the track. As they were pushed out and started one and two at a time on the front straight, I intensely studied each car.

What struck me the most was how much larger the right rear tire was than the left, and the word "stagger" became a new addition to my vocabulary. Stagger is the difference in circumference between the two tires, which helps the car turn in the corners. Picture rolling a Styrofoam cup on a table and how it rolls in a circle, and that's basically how stagger works.

My jaw dropped once again after flagman Doug Clark waved the green flag for the first set of hot laps for the sprint class. One after another the cars glided through turns three and four, their front tires twitched left and right to maintain traction and control, and then they were instantly on the front straightaway. Their top wings reflected the glaring sun and created wisps of vapor trail as they squeezed moisture out of the humid Iowa air. The cars streaked past us in a blur of color and sound.

I soon found out why we sat in Section B, as that was approximately the point where the drivers started pointing their cars to the left and appeared to pitch them nearly backwards into turn one. Sticky black mud clods flew through and over the catch fence and landed just a few rows in front of us. The continuous roar of the engines rang in my ears.

At that point, I was hooked. After the conclusion of that set of hot laps my brother-in-law leaned over, almost apologetically, and explained that the track was still greasy (slick) and the cars' speeds would increase later on in the evening.

It gave me goose bumps when Tim Trier, one of the track announcers at the time, exclaimed, "It's race time in the valley!" and, "It's showtime!" as the field of cars picked up the pace rolling through turns three and four in anticipation of the drop of the green flag for the features.

The races were close and it seemed no time before the leaders were in lapped traffic. I don't remember much else about that night, except I had entered a world I previously did not know existed, and I now knew what I was going to be doing on summer Saturday nights for the foreseeable future.

I believe Tod Bishop won that night, with a young Danny Lasoski finishing second. I say "believe" because for years I could have sworn that Danny Lasoski won the first race I ever attended at Knoxville, which would have made for a slightly more memorable memory. I thought this until Knoxville Raceway began publishing historical results on their website and I learned that Lasoski did not win a feature at the track in 1985. Darn facts.

Little did I know as I watched my first race at Knoxville that the second-place finisher would go on to become the winningest driver in the track's history. The Dover, Missouri, resident tallied 112 feature wins, 11 track championships, and four Nationals titles by the end of 2017.

I attended my first Knoxville Nationals that year and discovered my all-time favorite driver in winner Doug Wolfgang. The red, white, and blue Weikert's Livestock #29 the Sioux Falls, South Dakota, native and former track champion drove that year will always be the first thing that comes to mind when I picture a sprint car.

Knoxville welcomed Wolfgang back home in June of the following summer and he reinforced his legend status during a special night they called "Return of the Wolf." The track lured him from the tough and lucrative Pennsylvania circuit by tempting him with a $10,000 bonus if he could start at the tail of two heats, the dash, and the feature, and win each of them. And he did it - in addition to setting quick time during time trials.

The previous Wednesday night Wolfgang was in Knoxville and raced against the World of Outlaws, which is the premier sprint car sanctioning body on earth. That night I obtained my first ever driver autograph from him and remember being starstruck while nervously shaking his hand. I immediately regretted saying something unimaginative, like, "I'll be rooting for you on Saturday."

I stood and cheered Wolfgang on a few years later when he competed in "The Big Three Match Race" at Knoxville. The unique race was held on Independence Day during a show promoted by the upstart United Sprint Association (USA), which was a short-lived rival to the World of Outlaws.

Steve Kinser, from Bloomingtion, Indiana, Sammy Swindell, then from Bartlett, Tennessee, and Wolfgang were (and still are) known as "The Big Three" - due to their domination of the sport for several years. The trio combined for 1,224 World of Outlaws wins (and God only knows how many non-Outlaws feature victories), 23 World of Outlaws championships, and 18 Knoxville Nationals championships during their careers. (While Kinser and Wolfgang have retired, these numbers could change. Swindell, in his sixties, was still racing selected events through the end of 2017.)

The format was consecutive three lap match races with the cars starting three-abreast. They rotated the pole position for each race – with the pole sitter moving to the middle slot, middle car moving to the outside, and outside to the pole after each race. The first driver to win two of the races picked up a $5,000 check.

It couldn't have worked out better if the promoters had scripted it. The pole was the fast line around the track at that point of the night and Wolfgang had that spot for the first race. He took full advantage of it and won. Kinser won the second and Swindell the third when they each had their turn to start from the pole.

For the fourth race Wolfgang shuffled back to the pole for the second time. There may have been a little gamesmanship going on as there were two false starts for this final race, possibly due to drivers jumping or hanging back on the starts. Once the green flag stayed out Wolfgang gained the lead and the victory, after an exciting moment when the second-running Kinser mounted a charge but got a little loose coming out of turn two.

In the post-race interview Tim Trier asked Wolfgang if he had ever started a race three-abreast before. Wolfgang said he thought he had in Australia once, but it didn't matter much because it was raining during that race.

Wolfgang went on to win the regular USA main event that night too.

I continued attending races at Knoxville in the summer of 1986, dragging along friends I worked with at a part-time job at a campground in Altoona. One Saturday night after the races were rained out, a friend and I decided to attend a going-away party in Altoona. The get-together was thrown for another friend who had joined the Army and was getting ready to ship off for boot camp.

Across the street lived a guy by the name of John Allen. He was a couple of years older than me and I knew him mostly as an acquaintance, since we both participated on the wrestling team back in high school. A boisterous and larger-than-life kind of guy, and not one to miss a party, especially one just across the street, John invited himself over.

We started talking and I mentioned I had just left Knoxville because the races were rained out. Talking further I found out that John used to attend the races at Knoxville regularly with his parents several years ago. It had been a while since he had attended a race and he missed it, so we made plans to go the next weekend.

Little did I know the future ramifications for me from that chance conversation, caused by a rain out.

For the next several years John and I rarely missed a race. Our interest in sprint cars grew in leaps and bounds as we got to know this niche in the world of racing.

We went to the races early and stayed late. We attended racing memorabilia auctions, charity benefits, driver softball games, and pretty much anything else that gave us an excuse to be in Knoxville. For a time our weekly race schedule consisted of watching ESPN's *Thursday Night Thunder*, Friday night races at the Iowa State Fair Speedway, Saturday nights at Knoxville, and maybe watching the NASCAR race on TV on Sundays. We became almost amateur weathermen, paying close attention to the forecast as race day drew near, as if our interest could somehow prevent a rain out.

I subscribed to *Open Wheel Magazine*, the then weekly *National Speed Sport News*, and the short-lived *Sprint Car* publication. I picked up a weekly track program, and the various local race papers that came and went over the years which were handed out at the track. I searched for any other sprint car related reading material I could find in order to feed my growing addiction.

It became obvious that we wanted to become involved in the sport. Really, as I sat in the stands, I just wanted to at least know somebody - anybody - involved in the sport.

My brother-in-law, an auto body technician by trade, happened to work at a Des Moines car dealership with a man named Mike Twedt. Mike was a very successful mini-sprint driver in central Iowa in those days. The mini-sprint he raced was a much smaller version of a sprint car, had similar suspension, and was powered by a souped-up snowmobile engine.

It seems that Mike's talents caught the eye of legendary Des Moines sprint car builder Bob Trostle. In 1987 Mr. Trostle partnered with Mike and his father to run a limited sprint car at Knoxville.

Here was my chance to become a little more involved, or at least know somebody who was involved, in the sport. Through my brother-in-law, John and I got to know Mike and his family and crew, and it gave us even more reason to go to the races.

By then we had moved to Section C in the stands, where Mike had quite a boisterous following. I'd like to apologize to those unfortunate folks who sat around us at the time. Sometimes our exuberance bordered, trampled on top of, and crossed the line to being obnoxious. Again, sorry about that. Going to the races and cheering for your favorite driver is one thing, but if you personally know that driver I think it can cause you to step it up a notch. Or several notches.

We witnessed first-hand the trials and tribulations of owning and operating a sprint car. The joys of winning, and the disappointment of coming up short. The hard work and time it takes to field a car, and the high cost involved. The fear of seeing someone you know crash one of these wicked vehicles, and then seeing him laid up in the hospital.

It didn't take long for John to become somewhat of a sponsor for Mike. I don't know exactly how much money John spent, but to this day he jokingly gripes about it once in a while. I only made a small donation a couple of times. Once when John, Brad Watson (a former pit crew member of Mike's who we became friends with), and I pooled some funds together to donate to the team after a crash. If I remember right it was enough to replace the top wing. On the other occasion I chipped in with several others to buy Mike a new driving suit. I was elated when he painted my name on the top of the hood of his car.

Other than that my involvement was limited to occasionally making the trek from Runnells to Mike's home in Huxley to help polish the car, which in my mind was a thrill at the time.

Mike's were the most beautiful sprint cars I have ever seen. He sprayed the car himself with a candy-apple red base, yellow, orange, and red stripes, and bright yellow frame. Numbers and lettering were applied with paint instead of stuck on vinyl. He added a shadowy silhouette portrait of Jesse James on both sides of the hood, and topped it all off with a coat or two of clear. There were very few stickers attached to the wing and body panels. His first car wore Trostle's famous #20, and thereafter the family #2T. His cars could be considered show cars, and he sometimes entered them in the annual car show held at the old Veterans Memorial Auditorium in Des Moines.

On one occasion I helped Mike and a few volunteers with unloading and rolling his car into an Oskaloosa mall for a little car show. Since it was held on a Saturday, with races at Knoxville that night, he needed some assistance to meet the schedule. I took some photos of his car inside the mall and submitted them to *Open Wheel Magazine*, along with - looking back now - a very cheesy write-up. I was thrilled when they published one of the photos and the write-up a few months later in the "In-Out Box" section of the magazine, which was their version of "letters to the editor."

We had a great deal of fun following Mike and his team, mostly because he was pretty successful and a heck of a likeable guy.

In addition to Knoxville we watched him race at Husets Speedway in South Dakota, and the Cheater's Day race at the state fairgrounds speedway in the same state.

We followed him to the quarter-mile bullring in Marshalltown, Iowa, where you could almost reach out and touch the cars going by on the front stretch. It was there where we watched a rut develop in the track that was as deep as the width of a clipboard. I only know that because John measured it with one during a red flag after another driver caught hold of said rut and flipped his sprint car in turn four. The car ended up outside the track with the front end atop a fence post, giving new meaning to the words "pole position." I believe that was the last time they allowed sprint cars at that racetrack.

We followed Mike to Boone, Iowa, and watched him win the most unusual of races. It pitted stock cars, modifieds, late models, and sprint cars against each other, all on the track at the same time.

To make the race competitive the sprints had to start the feature a lap down and at the tail of the field, due to their significantly greater speeds when compared to the stock car classes. In general, the modifieds were faster than stock cars, late models faster than modifieds, and sprint cars faster than late models. They lined the feature up with the slower vehicles at the front and worked their way to the fastest in the rear.

There were some concerns when this race was conceived because the lightweight sprint cars appeared dainty when compared to the much heavier stock car classes. Some sprint car teams went so far as to mount beefed up nerf bars on the sides of their cars, just for the added protection. Some also installed brakes on all four wheels of their sprint cars in an effort to make them behave more like a stock car while braking. Normally sprint cars only had one brake on the left front wheel and an inboard on the rear axle.

It was awfully entertaining to watch the sprint cars come from a lap down and the rear of the field. They put on a clinic slicing and dicing through traffic on the tight, high-banked quarter-mile track – passing the different classes of stock cars left and right, all the while battling against the other sprint cars in the race.

The concept of this race was ingenious as it automatically created a rivalry and a fight for bragging rights between the classes and their fans, which was bound to increase ticket sales.

One year upon exiting his sprint car in the pits after finishing this race, a victorious Fran Bruns exclaimed, "We showed those f*****s who's fast!"

We watched Mike at the state fairgrounds track in Des Moines, the track in Oskaloosa, and one I can't remember the name and location anymore. Wherever that was you could actually stick your head through the fence along the back straight and watch the cars race straight towards you. You had to protect your personal parts though, as one of our friends found out after taking a dirt clod to the crotch.

We followed him to Moberly, Missouri, where I caught an excellent shot on video of how Mike became involved in an accident. Unfortunately I cued the tape to show him the replay later, only to forget that fact at the start of the next race and I inadvertently taped over the footage.

We were thrilled to see him lead half of a heat race during one Knoxville Nationals, competing with his 360 cubic inch engine against the 410's - something unheard of even then. He led until his efforts were stopped short when the front wing mounts to his top wing failed, and the wing flopped over backwards like a toupee in a strong wind. He somehow kept the car on all fours, but the malfunction ended his run. Danny Lasoski was in that heat race and was rumored to say they would not have caught Mike's 360 had the wing mounts held together.

I visited Mike at Knoxville Community Hospital one time, where he was admitted for a spell after suffering a cracked vertebra due to a crash at the track. The crash didn't appear horrible, as his car spun around and did a slow backflip. The problem was that the car landed in one of the worst possible ways, with the bottom of the frame hitting the ground flat and causing his spine to compress. Compression fractures like these are why helicopter seats come equipped with shock absorbers. His crash was like a slap in the face and a revelation that the sport can be ruthless. Thankfully he fully recovered and continued to race.

We got to know Mike's uncle, Mike Harris (who Mike was named after), and his brother Jim. You could count on one hand the number of races these two guys have missed since they started attending races at Knoxville in the 1950's. Okay, maybe two hands, but not many more than that.

They could tell you anything you ever wanted to know about sprint car racing. I would say they've forgotten more about racing than I'll ever know, but I don't believe they have forgotten anything. I had trouble remembering who won the previous week, but they could tell you who won a race 20 years ago. They kept meticulous records and seemed to study the sport.

Jim made a log of which driver drove what car, nationwide, every year, and it was printed annually in a national racing publication. Jim's son was called "TJ" with the "T" being short for "Thad" – after Hall of Fame driver Thad Dosher. Dosher was an extremely successful and popular driver who raced at Knoxville in the 60's and 70's.

These brothers are the epitome of sprint car fans. "Fans," short for "fanatics," really isn't the correct word. It doesn't do what they are justice. No matter how much I read or think I know, from magazines, books, social media, or whatever, they both tell me things about sprint car racing that I've never heard. I suppose it's something that happens from following the sport since the 1950's. They are a part of the sport.

One year John and I took a road trip with these brothers to the Kings Royal sprint car race held at Eldora Speedway near Rossburg, Ohio. Knoxville will always be my favorite track, but I have never seen a sprint car go faster than at Eldora. It was literally breathtaking. Carved out of Ohio dirt by legendary Hall of Fame inductee Earl Baltes (and now owned by Tony Stewart), at this half-mile track you nearly needed to crawl up the steep banking in order to exit the pits.

Back then the fast line was all the way at the top, with cars circling the track inches from the outside concrete wall. It was there while sitting on lawn chairs on the terraces outside of turn one where we watched Danny Lasoski nearly clear the fence in a nasty type of accident which Eldora is known for. I thought for a moment that he would land in our laps.

On the way home we stopped and visited the museum at the Indianapolis Motor Speedway and took a one lap tour around the track. That was neat, but as the dirt aficionado saying goes, there is nothing wrong with the track that a few feet of dirt wouldn't fix.

I think it was after Mike won the 1989 Limited Sprint Car points championship at Knoxville when John offered to become a part owner of the Twedt sprint car. I'm not sure how it went, but I believe John wanted some decision-making involvement with the team. Since Mike and his father already owned the car and didn't feel they needed any added decision-makers, they declined the offer. It was amicable, yet John still wanted more involvement.

At around that same time John began attending the Winter Dome races held in the Livestock Pavilion building on the Iowa State Fairgrounds during the sprint car off-season. These races were literally rough and tumble and sometimes a good example of holding a fight with races breaking out. They raced motorcycles, 3-wheelers, 4-wheelers, go-carts, cage carts, and probably several other vehicles that I don't remember, indoors on a small oval track during the winter months.

John went along with a friend of his who raced motorcycles. Since most of these racers know one another, it was there where John met Jerry Crabb. Jerry was an extremely successful motorcycle, 3-wheeler, 4-wheeler, and who knows what else racer in the Dome.

Jerry had raced a 410 cubic inch sprint car for a car owner a few times at Knoxville during the 1990 season. Not one to be intimidated by a challenge, he made his debut during the two-day spring World of Outlaws show. The first heat race he competed in was won by Jeff Swindell, followed by Stevie Smith and Steve Kinser – three legends of the sport.

Later on I remember hearing from long-time Knoxville 4-wheeler driver Dave Cornwell, whose job it was to push sprint cars to the staging area and wherever else they needed to go, that this car Jerry drove was the heaviest one he'd ever pushed. Needless to say, because in racing more weight equals less speed, Jerry's first experience in a sprint car left something to be desired.

Nonetheless, Jerry wanted to try it again and was planning to build a 360 cubic inch sprint car of his own for the 1991 season. This was the perfect opportunity for John to gain the involvement he wanted, so the two decided to team up on this new racing venture.

John asked if I would like to be on the pit crew. It didn't take long for me to provide him an answer. Since doing so would be a great way for me to become more involved in the sport too, I said, "Sure, what the heck."

"The Doctor"

I was 24 years old when Jerry brought his own sprint car to Knoxville in 1991, and he was exactly twice my age. At around 5'8" and in the 170 lb. range, he had a stocky build, worked out regularly, and was probably in better physical shape than half the drivers he competed against. Many of those drivers were young enough to be his sons.

He was bald in the classic male pattern baldness, but kept the remaining gray hair that ran from ear to ear around the back of his head approximately an inch or two in length. That, plus his gray bushy mustache, gave him somewhat the look of a mild-mannered grandfather.

He definitely did not act like a mild-mannered grandfather though, and later when he clipped what hair he had left very close to his scalp he looked more like a drill sergeant, which better suited his personality. In the 60's Jerry served a stint in the Army, and in the 80's joined the Naval Reserves, so I am sure he knew about drill sergeants. His demeanor made me think he learned something from those guys.

Think John Wayne in a sprint car movie.

I believe the best words to describe Jerry are "old school." He was definitely not like some of the more polished racers you see today, who spend time impressing sponsors and look to move on to higher classes of race cars. He often wore cut-off jeans to the races, along with t-shirts that sported funny sayings, such as, "I Suffer From CRS – Can't Remember Shit."

He possessed a charismatic, magnetic personality. At the same time he was fiercely independent, stubborn, didn't pay much attention to what others thought of him, wasn't about to be taken advantage of, and lived his life how he saw fit.

For instance, at one point he completed some extensive body work on his van. He did the work himself, it looked pretty good, and he was proud of the results. One day not long after finishing this work he went to a local establishment for his morning coffee, and parked where he could keep an eye on the van from within the restaurant.

A car pulled in next to the van and a kid popped open the passenger door - and dinged the side of the freshly painted van. Jerry flew out of the restaurant and gave the young man a good old-fashioned cussing out. The boy's grandfather, who turned out to be a rather large man, stepped out of the driver's side door and let Jerry know he didn't particularly care for the outburst. Jerry came home with a black eye that day, but not before getting his own licks in.

He was also known to occasionally use the push-bumper mounted at the front of his van to nudge passenger cars, in an effort to let their drivers know, in a non-verbal manner, that he didn't appreciate their driving styles. Sometimes he let them know for a city block.

In another example, one night at Knoxville Jerry parked his trailer outside the track near the pit entrance in an area which clearly irritated a track security guard. The security guard approached Jerry and told him he needed to move his rig. Jerry told the security guard to go do something to himself that isn't physically possible, and walked away. The security guard, stunned, asked a nearby member of the safety crew, "Who is this guy?"

The crewmember just chuckled and replied, "That's Jerry Crabb, he's old school."

Jerry began racing motocross in the 1960's and continued racing flat track motorcycles, 3-wheelers, 4-wheelers, and just about anything else with wheels well into the 90's – and his 3-wheeler into the 2010's.

He was very successful racing these vehicles but I don't know how many races he won, and I doubt he does either. A

TV repairman by trade, there was a storage room in a dark part of his shop on SW 9th which held what seemed to be hundreds of dusty trophies lined around the walls amongst a variety of motorcycle and TV parts.

I don't know what it is about TV repairmen, but the two I knew had nearly identical shops in the sense that they were, well, cluttered. They were clean, but basically there was a path to walk through amid an assortment of TV pieces in various stages of repair. In Jerry's case these parts shared space with an assortment of sprint car and motorcycle parts. Jerry had a partner at the time who worked on VCRs at the front of the building, so those parts were thrown into the mix as well.

There were numerous times I stopped by the shop to find Jerry hunched over his work table in the midst of this clutter, soldering on a circuit board or electrical wiring. Peering through the magnifying glass he had attached to a device he created which allowed him to maneuver the lens hands-free in all directions.

I don't know how old the building was that housed his shop, but my guess is it was built well before I was born. Maybe even before Jerry was born.

At one time Jerry devised a unique contraption to temporarily solve a leaking roof problem. It consisted of a large sheet of plastic stretched just beneath the ceiling. The center was pulled down somewhat to allow water running through the leak in the roof to pool in the middle of the plastic. In that spot was a hole to allow the water to pass through the plastic. Directly below that was a garbage can lid with a hole in the middle, turned upside down, which acted as a funnel. This passed the water to a PVC pipe that sloped and ran several feet, through a hole in the wall, and then dumped it outside. Even though it reminded me of something Wile E. Coyote might have designed, it worked.

Divorced and the father of two grown children out on their own, Jerry lived in the basement of his shop. Driving by the establishment you would never guess someone lived beneath the old building.

Surprisingly, it was a plush two-bedroom apartment which contained a living room, kitchen, and bathroom. Hanging from the ceiling next to a wall in the living room were three TV's, which I guess was appropriate for someone in the TV repair business. On the walls were a variety of awards and photos from previous racing accomplishments.

He also had a waterbed, weight set, and for a time a tanning bed down in his bachelor pad. A small wooden hand-made sign above the second step from the bottom of the stairs read, "Be careful, the third step is a bitch." Unfortunately that warning did not always help the uninitiated when they stepped on that slanted third step.

Jerry's shop had an attached overhang instead of garage when he built his first sprint car. Since it was wintertime when he built the car he completed the assembly in a spare storage room in his shop. This was fine except for the fact that once the car was built it wouldn't fit through the double doors which led to the outside.

He knew this would be the case when he started building the car, and figured once completed he would simply remove the axles and enlist some volunteers to help carry it outside. Thankfully, after we sweated and struggled to squeeze the car through those doors, he decided to enclose the overhang and turned it into a fine garage.

The garage was furnished with cable TV (so Jerry could watch his beloved Chicago Cubs), a radio, workbench, shelves, tools, and refrigerator. The refrigerator was stocked with a variety of beer that John received from a friend who drove a beer truck. This friend would give John a discount on damaged cases of beer, which resulted in many confused looks whenever a dented can of beer was handed to someone stopping by the shop or by our pit stall after the races.

A flood light activating motion detector was installed on the outside of the garage in an attempt to discourage any potential petty thieves who roamed the area. On one occasion an industrious thief pried some siding off the outside of the garage and cut his way through the wall. The thief apparently didn't know what he was doing as he overlooked a fairly expensive set of heads that were sitting out in the open. Jerry kept a shotgun handy just in case he was confronted by one of these punks, but thankfully never had to use it.

I have warm memories of that garage and it was there where Jerry taught me what I know about sprint cars. Early on in his sprint car career I would stop by after work a night or two during the week and help maintain the car. He showed me how to clean injectors, pack bird-cage bearings, change torsion bars, block a car, square a rear end, groove, sipe, and mount tires, and perform other basic sprint car maintenance tasks.

Once in a while I even got to help him change engines. On more than one occasion the car sat almost totally disassembled on the floor, in the midst of repair following an accident from the previous weekend.

There is just something nice about working on a race car into the evening, TV or radio playing in the background, with the garage door wide open to let in the spring or summertime air.

Jerry was known for his ability to fabricate parts, and if he needed something and could come up with a way to make it, he would make it. The 3 and 4-wheelers he raced at the Winter Dome where handcrafted by him from scratch, and in my opinion could be considered works of art. These machines only resembled the machines he raced against in that they had three and four wheels, respectively, and handlebars. They were offset to the left and had welded tubular low-slung frames, small wheels and tires, and polished aluminum gas tanks.

Jerry was somewhat of a legend at the Winter Dome races and regularly held court in his enclosed trailer parked outside the arena on race night. The trailer was equipped with a kerosene heater to help fight off the frigid Iowa winters and warm the aching joints he had damaged from too many years of racing.

Visitors would come and go in a continuous stream throughout the night - looking for advice, seeking a spare part or tool they needed that they just knew Jerry would have, or simply old friends stopping by to catch up and wish him well.

Since the Winter Dome track was very small it caused a lot of unintentional and intentional contact between machines. This sometimes caused tempers to rise, so Jerry kept a large inch and a quarter wrench handy in case it would be necessary for something other than turning a large nut. Thankfully I don't think he ever needed to use it.

Somewhere down the line a track announcer tabbed Jerry with the nickname "The Doctor." I don't know why, and neither does Jerry. He even asked the announcer where the nickname came from, but didn't receive a straight answer.

Could it be because he is a TV repairman, therefore a TV doctor? That seems sort of silly. Maybe it's because he had been around so long and was one of a dwindling number of drivers who knew how a sprint car was put together and how it worked, and answered questions from drivers new to the sport, therefore making him a sprint car PhD? That is also a stretch. Or possibly because his body had suffered many years of racing-related abuse, he walked with a slight limp, and presumably spent a lot of time in doctors' offices? Maybe.

When asked how he got the nickname Jerry usually replied that he was the "Dr. of Love."

Yes, Jerry was definitely old school and had seen almost everything in racing. But I don't think he knew what he bargained for as far as a pit crew was concerned when he teamed up with John on his own sprint car venture in 1991.

A Cast of Characters

To say we were green at the time would be an understatement. I had worried about my inexperience somewhat ever since John asked me to help on the pit crew, but evidently not too much because I was pretty excited on opening night. I guess ignorance really is bliss, until you try to do something that you really don't know how to do. I found out right away that there were going to be many opportunities to make myself look like an idiot.

As I stood there in our pit stall that first night at Knoxville, feeling very self-conscious and wondering what the heck I was supposed to do, Jerry thrust some plastic zip ties into my hand and told me to, "Put these on the shocks."

"Okay," I replied. I had no idea what he was talking about. Rather than ask for an explanation, since Jerry did not seem to be in an explaining mood, I went to John and asked for his opinion. He had no idea either.

Brad Watson was nearby so I asked him. He explained to me that sometimes a zip tie is tied around the shaft that travels up and down in the shock. Before the car goes out onto the track the zip tie, with the excess end clipped off, is slid up to the body of the shock. As a load is placed on the shock and the shaft moves up and down in the body, the zip tie is pushed down the shaft and remains there, and will provide an idea of how far the shaft traveled up and down, therefore a better understanding of the setup.

I realized I might be in trouble here.

Nonetheless I soldiered on and placed the zip ties on the shocks. A little later when Jerry was standing nearby I verified with him that I did what he wanted me to do with the zip ties. He confirmed this and then asked, "Didn't you used to crew for Twedt?"

Obviously what we had here was a failure to communicate.

I informed him that I was, basically, just a fan, but wanted to learn and help out. With a grimaced look of impatience he shook his head, turned away, and continued about his business. Apparently John had not filled Jerry in on our qualifications, or lack thereof.

I had a lot to learn.

There are no hard and fast rules regarding the size, duties, or experience level of a sprint car pit crew, and these attributes can vary greatly from team to team. They can range anywhere from only the driver and any bystanders he can grab to help him push the car out of his pit stall, all the way to totaling the allotted number of pit passes the track allows, plus several other hangers-on.

They are nothing like the crews you see in NASCAR or IndyCar, as far as wearing fireproof suits and helmets and performing speedy scheduled pit stops on pit lane. There are many better-funded sprint car teams where the crews wear snazzy matching shirts and pants, but there are also those who appear to have just stepped off the set of the old TV show *Hee-Haw*.

Some highly-funded professional crews have individuals designated as crew chiefs, car chiefs, tire specialists, and other areas they can distinguish – with more members based in the home shop - but not always. Many crews consist of family members and friends of the driver and/or car owner. Some are made up of anyone who is willing to volunteer their time for the sheer joy of being included on a sprint car team, and duties vary based on what the driver needs completed.

I'd say Jerry's crew consisted of the latter.

In the early years of his sprint car career Jerry would grin and tell people his pit crew consisted of a bartender, plumber, bricklayer, and computer programmer. I think the people he told this to believed he was pulling their leg. In fact, he was right on the money. The original crew was Ron Nelson, John, Scott Veach, and me.

Ron Nelson was the bartender.

We simply called him Nelson, but Jerry eventually started calling him Norton, in reference to the Norton character from *The Honeymooners* TV show - both in appearance and actions. For a while Jerry had "Norton" printed on the car under the pit crew section in place of Nelson's given name.

Nelson resembled a cross between Kramer from *Seinfeld* and the aforementioned Norton. He regularly wore a red collared Polo type shirt to the races, which bore a small "CRABB 12x" in black block lettering on the front breast pocket, and another huge "CRABB 12x" that covered the back.

A sort of goofy but lovable, interesting character, Nelson would sometimes make folksy and understated comments such as, "Those are some fast puppies," when we watched a World of Outlaws race when they were in town.

A former motocross racer, in his younger days Nelson once loaded up his bike and headed to a race in Missouri all by himself. While there he was involved in a particularly nasty crash, which caused a great deal of pain in his chest and left him with temporary limited use of his arms. He somehow loaded his bike and made his way back to Des Moines. Once home he went to the doctor and found he had torn many of the muscles in his chest.

He also proudly told me on more than one occasion that he once owned a clothing store in Des Moines which contained the city's first adult entertainment shop in a back room. I'm not sure how a person would go about completing a fact-check on this information, so I'll take him at his word.

At the time he helped on Jerry's pit crew, Nelson was a bartender in the upscale Des Moines restaurant located at the top of 801 Grand, the tallest building in the state.

He had known Jerry since the 70's, when they both raced motocross. He took credit (blame?) for Jerry's immersion into racing. Nelson raced motocross in the 60's, along with a few flat track events. By the early 70's he was in the process of winding down his racing activities, but still ran an occasional race now and then.

Nelson's father tinkered in Jerry's TV shop on the south side of Des Moines from time to time. One day he called his son and asked if Crabb could borrow one of Nelson's motorcycles to race in an upcoming show at the Warren County Fairgrounds - a race that Nelson had also planned to participate in.

He had to ponder the question for a moment. At the time he had never met Crabb and didn't know he had any previous racing experience. But he had driven by the TV shop before and saw a street bike parked outside, so figured Crabb could at least drive in a straight line.

"Sure," Nelson told his father, "why not?"

"Crabb didn't do all that well in that race," Nelson once told me with a twinkle in his eye, "but he won the wheelie contest."

Although I always felt he knew more about racing than the credit he received, Nelson turned making himself the object of Jerry's scorn and contempt into an art form. Mostly this occurred whenever he held a wrench in his hand. It seemed that whatever he was doing - changing a tire, replacing a shock, tightening a bolt, speaking, just standing there, whatever - Jerry had to give him grief for not doing it right. Jerry was definitely the Ralph Kramden to Nelson's Norton.

Jerry's feelings did not come totally without warrant. One of my favorite stories involving Nelson happened during a race at the Iowa State Fairgrounds, on a night when I was absent. It seems they did some work on the engine which required them to remove the coil wire.

After the push truck pushed Jerry around the track a few times in an unsuccessful attempt to start the car for the feature, Jerry finally pulled into the pits located outside the track.

Back at the pit stall there Nelson stood, sporting a sheepish expression, with the coil wire dangling from his hand.

I still hear this story now and then, and how Nelson held that coil wire high in the air every time the push truck pushed Jerry's car by his position next to the fence.

Nelson was dependable though, and spent a lot of time at the shop. If he was expected to be there, he was there, and I believe deep down Jerry appreciated his help.

One weekend Jerry needed to be in Chicago Saturday morning to attend his son's graduation from college. This caused a logistics dilemma because of the Friday night races at the Iowa State Fair Speedway, and then the Saturday night races in Knoxville. The plan was for Jerry to take my car Friday night after the races at the fairgrounds and head for Chicago. I'd take the van, trailer, and race car to my home in Runnells, and then we'd meet up in Knoxville Saturday night after he returned from the graduation.

Unfortunately, Jerry's sprint car stripped the cam spud on Friday night. This is a little piece of metal that serves as a link between the engine cam and the fuel pump. This is one of those proverbial 25 cent parts that if fails can shut down the entire operation (not really, nothing on a sprint car only costs 25 cents).

The problem was that Jerry didn't have a spare cam spud, no one at the track had one, and he had no time to pick up a replacement and fix the car the next day since he was leaving immediately after the races. So it was up to Nelson and me to get the job done.

This caused Jerry a certain amount of consternation.

He went over what we needed to do several times. He described how to remove the fuel pump, how to install it, where to purchase the part, etc., over and over again. He finally took the pump off to eliminate at least one step that we could potentially screw up the next day.

It was clear to me he did not have a great deal of confidence in our abilities. Jerry reluctantly left in my car and headed for Chicago, and Nelson and I made arrangements to meet back at Jerry's shop the next morning to fix the car.

By the time I arrived at the shop the next morning, Nelson was already waiting. We quickly washed the car, went and bought the part, came back to the shop and replaced the stripped one, and then each headed home. It definitely wasn't a difficult job, but still it went better than expected. Jerry need not have worried. We all met at Knoxville on Saturday night without incident.

Nelson was always like this, always there when needed. Whether washing the mud off the car early in the morning after a night of racing, making a trip to pick up fuel, helping to pull the engine, or anything else that needed to be done, it didn't matter, he would be there.

After several years, one day Nelson just stopped showing up. I never found out if something specific happened or if he just grew tired of the whole racing scene.

By chance I saw him a few years later in a doctor's office. He said he had attended the races at Knoxville a few times since leaving the team, sat in the stands, and watched us working down in the pits through his binoculars. But he didn't stop by our pit stall after the races and had no desire to return to our pit crew. I find this hard to believe, because once racing is in your blood it is usually difficult to get it out.

I later heard that he and his wife were going to buy a houseboat and live in it off the coast of Florida. I don't know if that ever happened, but would not be surprised if it did.

John was the plumber.

He was a big guy in high school, at over 6' tall and wrestling in the 189 lb. weight class. Years of manual labor as a plumber following high school put him at well over 200. He was strong and solid and held a few stints as a bouncer in local bars. He owned one of those huge black MAGLITE flashlights that policemen carried, and once showed me the marks it wore which were the result of it coming into contact with the teeth of patrons he had previously bounced.

I knew he had been in fights before, but throughout all the years I was around him I never once saw him get into a fight. I had witnessed instances come close, but the other guy would always back down. Probably a smart move on the other guy's part.

He had the best eyesight of anyone I know. Anytime I rode with him he would always point out deer, pheasants, turkeys, or any other animal well before anyone else could see them. Sometimes I never could see them, but he could.

I usually preferred to drive though, because I think his superior vision encouraged him to gawk at everything but the road. On the occasions he drove I found myself putting my foot through an imaginary brake on the floorboard of the passenger side, and had to resist reaching over and grabbing the wheel as we occasionally drifted over the center line.

His size and thick blonde hair made him resemble John Daly, the golfer, in Mr. Daly's slimmer days. Other golfers sometimes voiced that comparison when John was on the golf course, until he launched a ball off the tee in an impressive slice. His golf balls might travel as far as John Daly's, but wouldn't always find the fairway he was playing.

John mostly played the role of car owner and never seemed too interested in the mechanical side of things. With the number of plumbing side jobs and other activities he participated in, he simply didn't have a lot of time to deal with car maintenance.

He liked the strategy of racing, and had the ability to look at issues from every angle and formulate decisive resolutions. If something came up or a question arose that we didn't have the answer to, John would be on the phone immediately. It seemed he had a Rolodex in his head which contained a list of contacts appropriate for any situation. He was unbelievably quick with numbers, possessed the memory of an elephant, and had the knack to win any argument.

One thing about John - he would not take crap from anyone, no matter who they were. One year during the Knoxville Nationals the pit crew of his all-time favorite driver, Sammy Swindell, made an attempt to manually move Mike Twedt's open sprint car trailer. They tried to do this so they could move Sammy's semi and enclosed trailer, which was parked outside the track, and Mike's trailer was in their way. This sort of ticked off the Twedt crew and John found out about the incident.

Later that night after the races we saw Sammy driving his own semi pulling his trailer into the pit area. John walked over, climbed the steps to the passenger side of the semi, opened the door, and took a seat in the cab next to Sammy.

It seems they had a little discussion, and John voiced his displeasure over the actions of Sammy's crew. Sammy ensured John that he would have a talk with his crew. I do not know if Sammy had that talk with his crew guys, but I would imagine he felt somewhat threatened when this big blonde-headed guy crawled up into the cab of his semi.

Another time before we started helping on Jerry's pit crew,

John, my brother-in-law, my cousin, and I went to the races in Knoxville. It had rained recently and there was a large mud puddle in the middle of the pits. After the races and a few adult beverages, John and my brother-in-law became involved in a friendly little spat over a topic insignificant enough that I do not remember what it was about.

The spat escalated to the point where the two ended up in a wrestling match in the middle of that mud puddle. At one point my brother-in-law was lying on his back in the mud, while John sat on top of him. My brother-in-law bravely (stupidly?) picked up a glob of mud in each hand while a very mischievous grin spread across his face.

John warned him, "Don't even think about it, you'll be sorry."

He did not heed the warning and John took both handfuls of mud, one on either side of his face. My brother-in-law insists it was worth it, but I do not believe him. They both ended up covered from head to toe in mud, but my brother-in-law definitely got the worst of it.

The point is, John and my brother-in-law are friends. You could joke with John to a point, but you did not want to come close to crossing any sort of line. I spent several quarters in the old car wash outside turn two that night, spraying mud off of those two guys before allowing them to set foot in my car.

John was a perfect example of a big guy with a heart of gold. After I bought a piece of land I took him there to show him my purchase. I was contemplating building a manufactured home at the time, but John immediately deduced that I could contract a stick built home myself more economically using the contacts he had made over the years as a plumber.

By the time we left my land that day John already had in mind who would dig the basement (Detrick Excavating, one of our sponsors, of course) and pour the foundation and sidewalk. Who would frame, roof, and install electrical and HVAC. Who would drywall, trim, paint, install the septic system, and trench the water and gas line. Obviously John would do the plumbing work.

In essence, he offered to act as my contractor. He lined everyone up and never took a penny for it, other than what I paid him for the plumbing work he completed. I would not have been able to build my house without him, and for that I will forever be in his debt.

John's big booming voice was a staple in our pit area, and he could sling good-natured crap with the best of them. Wherever you went with John, and I mean it could be anywhere in the country, he always seemed to run into people he knew.

After a few years with Jerry, John went a different and more economical route with his involvement in racing by becoming a 4-wheeler driver at Knoxville. Incidentally the first car John ever pushed with a 4-wheeler at Knoxville was Steve Kinser, arguably the greatest sprint car driver of all time.

"Arguably" isn't the right word, since it would be difficult to argue against. Kinser won the World of Outlaws point championship an astounding 20 times, including the inaugural 1978 season. He officially tallied 690 World of Outlaws feature victories during his career - which doesn't include who knows how many non-Outlaws features he won. He was also a 12-time Knoxville Nationals champion. They don't call him "The King" for nothing.

John had to push the car backwards for a short distance, and directed Kinser by hand signal regarding which way to turn. But Kinser didn't seem to trust the process, as he sat in the cockpit and continuously turned his head left and right in an effort to see behind him.

Afterwards John smirked and simply said, "Kinser doesn't like to go backwards."

John still stopped by our pit area regularly to give us grief and eat the snacks Jan provided. Later on Jerry occasionally acted as a plumber's helper for John on certain jobs. It would have been interesting to be a fly on the wall to see that.

Scott Veach was the bricklayer.

He was a high school classmate of mine who I didn't know very well until John invited him to join the pit crew. John got to know him because they had both dated the same woman for a time (but not at the same time). Something like that could have resulted in fisticuffs, but somehow they became friends because of it.

We called Scott "Smoothie" based on something that

happened one January when we attended the Chili Bowl Nationals indoor midget race in Tulsa, Oklahoma. We stayed at the Embassy Suites there due to a discount we received because John and Scott knew someone who worked for the hotel chain in Des Moines.

Embassy Suites offered free drinks for a couple of hours every afternoon, and we made sure we took advantage of their generous offer during our stay. It is possible we came out ahead on that deal.

One day before we headed to the races, John, Brad, Scott, and I sat around a table in the lobby enjoying the free beverages. John noticed a couple of pretty young ladies walking by and brought this bit of information to our attention. Scott then made an attempt to nonchalantly turn his head in order to take in the view of the pretty ladies.

I don't believe Scott knew the meaning of the word nonchalant, as we witnessed one of the worst displays in history of someone trying to be inconspicuous.

John simply said, "Smoooooooth."

I'm sure it had something to do with the free drinks, but John's comment struck us as terribly funny. From that day forward, Scott was known as Smoothie.

Smoothie, or Smooth for short, stood around 5'8" and weighed maybe 140 lbs., but was surprisingly strong due to working for his family's bricklaying business (he and his brother did the brickwork on my house). He had fairly long and curly reddish bushy hair that basically made him look like he had just woken up most of the time. He regularly wore big tinted glasses, like the ones worn by Hyde on *That 70's Show*, and was rarely seen without a cigarette dangling from his mouth.

At that point in time he liked to party. For a couple of summers we had a permanent tee time at a local golf course at the ridiculously early hour of 6:50 a.m. on Sunday mornings. This was definitely poor planning on our part, as we usually didn't arrive home from the races at Knoxville until well after midnight Sunday morning.

Smoothie didn't let this affect his partying though, and there was more than one occasion where we picked him up to go golfing and he was still in the same clothes and feeling the effects from the previous night's festivities.

I will never forget the time when he asked the person running the concession stand in the clubhouse at around 6:30 a.m. one Sunday morning, "Do you serve alcohol this early?" I'm not sure if he was supposed to, but the man just shrugged and said, "Sure, why not," and Smooth had a beer for breakfast. I imagine the man figured that if someone needed alcohol that bad, he better serve it to him.

One of the funniest things I have ever witnessed happened to Smooth on the golf course. He owned an enormous golf umbrella that was always attached to the side of his golf bag, and I don't believe he ever walked by his bag without mentioning how great this umbrella was. Continuous comments, such as, "Isn't my umbrella awesome?" and, "If it rains I sure know I'm not going to get wet," made us grow weary and collectively roll our eyes. He clearly had some sort of fixation on this umbrella.

One day a particularly nasty thunderstorm, common to the hot and humid Iowa summers, sprang up and caught us out on the golf course. It was extremely windy and the rain blew nearly horizontally. Brad and I threw our clubs in our bags, hopped in our cart, and headed for the side of a maintenance building near the fairway we were playing – with the hopes that the building would offer some protection from the storm. John had the same idea and jumped in his cart, and hollered at Smooth to do the same.

But alas, this was Smooth's big moment to prove the worthiness of his awesome umbrella. He deftly pulled it from his bag in a motion that reminded me of a sword fighter drawing his sword.

John shook his head, gave Smoothie the "you're an idiot" look, and quickly drove his cart next to ours and in the protection of the maintenance building.

This is where the show started, and we had front row seats.

In the driving rain and already soaked to the bone, Smooth tried in vain to open his umbrella. He tried facing into the wind, then away from the wind, while cussing and fiddling with the mechanism that should allow the umbrella to open. Head down and beginning to look like a drowned rat, he continued to wrestle with his precious umbrella.

Finally, after several moments of trying, he hit the magic combination which unfolded his prized possession. Fortunately for us, not so for him, he was facing downwind when the umbrella opened.

Predictably, the umbrella immediately turned inside out. Undaunted, Smooth quickly turned into the wind in an attempt to right his wayward umbrella. But the wind caught it, turned him sideways, and the umbrella turned inside out once again. Much to our amusement this action repeated itself for several more moments, until many of the metal wires that were supposed to support the canopy stuck out in several wrong directions.

Finally, after resigning himself to imminent defeat, Smooth stopped his thrashing and looked down at the damaged, precious umbrella he held in his hand.

Suddenly a flash of rage came over his face and you could see the anger build within him. At that moment he grasped the handle with both hands, held the umbrella high over his head, and began slamming that poor thing into the ground, over and over. After pieces of his pride and joy began to scatter around him, he finally gave the umbrella one final slam to the ground and left its twisted, torn, and broken form lying in the wet grass.

Still in the pouring rain he stood back and looked down at the umbrella carcass for a moment, hands on his hips, soggy cigarette hanging from his mouth, and evidently decided he had not received his full revenge from this traitor. It was then that he began stomping its remains into the ground, over and over, until the poor thing was imbedded in the soft, rain-soaked earth. He then slowly, silently, and without emotion, turned and made his way to our carts.

Of course John, Brad, and I thought this entire episode was hilarious. And we never had to hear about that umbrella again, except of course when we brought up the subject of its demise, which occurred regularly.

A separate humorous episode conducted by Smooth happened on the 18th hole of the very same golf course. After two consecutive worm-burning drives, each hitting the same pile of rocks several yards in front of the tee box, his ball dribbled farther behind us after each attempt.

The third time was the charm, however John, Brad, and I had a difficult time finishing the round due to tears of laughter clouding our vision. Ironically Smooth was a really good golfer, his whole family participated in the sport, and his father was a member of a local private golf course.

Smooth was a live wire and had a high amount of energy. He was inquisitive and eager to learn and make himself useful. When something needed to be done, for example changing a tire, it seemed that he must have thought it was a race to beat you to the wheel wrench. He felt the need to be in the middle of everything.

He could talk trash with the best of them, and could cuss a blue streak that would make a Navy veteran proud. He was fun to have around. Like Nelson, Smooth just stopped showing up one day. But in his case it was due to marriage, which can sometimes put the kibosh on folks' racing activities.

I was the computer programmer. Even though I was not a programmer at the time, Jerry knew I worked with computers and figured that was close enough. Strange that I actually did become a programmer several years later, but I digress.

Karl Kinser, one of the greatest sprint car mechanics of all time, I am not. In fact, the only thing I can think of that I have in common with him is that we've both touched a sprint car.

But I guess I did have the passion and willingness to try. It really doesn't take much talent to scrape mud off the car or change a tire, shock, or gears, and generally I at least made an attempt to do what I was told.

That, plus the fact that my services came cheap (Jerry gave me a pit pass and I paid my own way in, but I did get to eat handfuls of the Hot Tamales and peanut M&M's Jan provided), are the main reasons I wasn't told to leave the pit premises. I am grateful, for there are not many opportunities in life to be involved with something you really love to do.

Over the years there were several others who turned wrenches for periods of time on Jerry's #12x sprint car. One of the earliest was John DeMoss, who is probably the only person besides Jerry who really knew what he was doing on our pit crew at the time. I think Jerry turned in some of his best performances while John helped, and I have a newspaper clipping from that period showing Jerry as high as eighth in points at Knoxville, which wasn't too shabby.

Earl Terry would lend a helping hand now and then. Earl liked to spend time on the slot machines at Prairie Meadows Racetrack and Casino, and at one point stated he did so well there that he could not remember a time when he had so much money. I do not know if that lasted. Earl had some racing knowledge and liked to offer his opinion on car setups and the like, which Jerry did not always entertain. Jerry's voicing of his opinion in disagreement with these suggestions I'm guessing is why Earl didn't stick around regularly.

Jeff Morris helped out for a while also, and it was Jeff's 410 cubic inch engine that Jerry used in a temporary attempt to race in that class and qualify for the Knoxville Nationals one year.

Jeff had been around the sport a long time, helped several teams over the years, and knew the racing scene quite well. He also spent some time wrenching on a second car Jerry built which was driven for a few years by Mark Detrick, one of our sponsors.

On one occasion another driver was using one of Jeff's engines, and Jeff decided that Jerry was going to use this engine. Unfortunately that driver wasn't aware of this bit of information until the day Jeff and Jerry showed up at the driver's door to pull the engine out of his car.

There were some others who made brief appearances through the years, whose names I have either forgotten or never knew. A good example was that of a husband and wife schoolteacher couple Jerry met somewhere down the line who helped for several weeks.

They asked a ton of questions and seemed very eager to learn. One day they just stopped showing up. I don't know if something happened in their lives, or if they simply tired of burning up all of their Saturday nights in Knoxville.

In most of these cases Jan would tell any new helpers that I would train them on what to do. The training usually consisted of me telling them, "Uh, do whatever you want."

In later years the pit crew included Jan, Tracie Wilson, and her son Shane. Because of the two females Jerry's team was sometimes referred to as "The Women's Crew," much to Shane's and my chagrin.

Jan was the petite mother of two from a previous marriage, who had brunette hair sprinkled with gray. At the time she had been promoted from Jerry's girlfriend, to Jerry's fiancé, to Jerry's wife. "Promoted" is not really the correct word because, like Jerry, she was a person who lived life on her own terms and wouldn't have allowed anyone to "promote" her if it was not to her liking.

Incredibly kind and thoughtful, Jan weekly asked how my kids were doing and regularly had a story to tell about her grandchildren. She also made it a point to keep the trailer stocked with M&Ms, Mike & Ikes, Hot Tamales, and sometimes homemade assorted goodies. She even went so far as to make a batch of popcorn every week for the backstretch Knoxville Raceway Fire and Rescue Crew. I know they appreciated that because they always brought the bowl back empty.

A very strong-willed person, Jan seemed to have a weekly disagreement with the poor Knoxville Raceway infield official whose job was to post the lineups for each race. She was usually right about lineups as she meticulously kept records of each race, starting positions and all, and figured the lineups for the B and A features by hand. This was not a simple task since the track's complicated formula utilized points for finishing positions and passing cars, and she normally had that figured out before the official posted the lineups.

In another example of her character, one night it seems Jan and Jerry had some sort of disagreement before the races began. Jan decided she had had enough and chose to walk home to Des Moines from Knoxville, which is about a 40 mile jaunt.

Jerry let her go. An acquaintance met her outside the track, got the gist of what was going on, and offered to give her a ride home. She would have none of it. Later that night another acquaintance saw her walking in Pleasantville, around 10 miles away, and convinced her to accept a ride the rest of the way to Des Moines.

For a time Jan had the nickname "Pigpen" because of her willingness to jump right in on the mechanical side of things, not one bit afraid to get her hands dirty. Later on Jan mostly gave that up and concentrated on keeping her stats and lineups, and cleaned Jerry's helmet and installed its shield tear-offs. That and the several times a night when I needed to dodge her push broom as she swept dirt and grime out of the trailer that we had tracked in. Oh, and she was also in charge of the all-important, as Jerry called it, "driver morale."

Jan worked for a magazine publishing company in Des Moines and sometimes brought this work with her to the races. She also spent a great deal of time with Jerry working at the farm they purchased somewhere between Lacona and Chariton, where they moved a mobile home and planned to build a house. Moreover, Jan spent a fair amount of time trying to convince Jerry to give up this racing business – knowing that was likely a losing battle, and might even have the opposite effect. That was one discussion I stayed clear of.

However, she did experience firsthand the addiction affliction associated with sprint car racing. One year they held a flat track motorcycle race at Knoxville, and invited Jerry and Mark Detrick to bring their sprint cars down to help pack the track. Jan hopped in Jerry's car and took a few laps.

At one point, Mark passed Jan.

Jan picked up the pace.

Jan wanted to pass Mark back.

Back in the pits Jerry got on Jan's case a bit, and told her she was maybe going a little too fast. Jan told them, "Okay, I get it now – why you guys like racing these things – I get it."

At the time Tracie recently turned 40 and had attended races at Knoxville since she was a child. She got hooked up with Jerry through Jan, whose kids she used to baby sit. Dark haired and dark-complected, Jerry once had the name "Boobs Galore" printed on his car under the pit crew section in place of her given name. This was due to an obvious part of her anatomy.

A strong gal and anything but soft-spoken, it was not

unusual to see Tracie involved in minor skirmishes with Jerry, her son, or anyone foolish enough to give her grief - and to see those challengers regularly end up with the short end of the stick. You never saw me do this because I do not believe my ego could have handled my ass getting kicked by her.

A former "beer girl" at Des Moines Buccaneer hockey games, and a "Volunteer of the Year" for the popular Iowa Games, Tracie was never afraid to speak to anybody and had the knack for making friends with everyone she met.

Tracie once told me about an occurrence at a Des Moines restaurant where she spotted a patron wearing a Terry McCarl racing t-shirt. Tracie walked up to the man and said, "Hey, Terry McCarl sucks."

Terry McCarl, a very well-known Iowa sprint car driver, seems to have raced at Knoxville Raceway since the dawn of time. Born into a racing family, his father Lenard, uncle Ivan, brother Kenny, nephew Kyle, and sons Austin and Carson, have all turned laps in a sprint car at Knoxville.

With 58 victories by the end of 2017, Terry sits third on the all-time 410 class feature win list at Knoxville Raceway – two wins behind Doug Wolfgang and one ahead of Steve Kinser. A seven-time Knoxville track champion, he has qualified for 21 Nationals A mains and finished in the top 10 in that race multiple times. Throw in seven 360 class feature wins, including four 360 Knoxville Nationals championships. He holds track records at Knoxville up the ying-yang. He has experienced success racing sprint cars all across the country, and owns 13 World of Outlaws feature victories. In 2017 he was inducted into the National Sprint Car Hall of Fame.

Clearly, Terry McCarl does not "suck." Sometimes Tracie just likes to stir things up.

Tracie and the man conversed in the restaurant for a while, laughing and talking racing, until who walks in and sits down with the man but none other than Terry McCarl himself.

The man, thinking he had her in a tight corner, said to Tracie, "Are you going to say now what you said a minute ago?"

She just replied, "What, that Terry McCarl sucks? Sure, why not?"

I think they all got a laugh out of that.

When Tracie was honored for being the volunteer of the year for the Iowa Games she spent two hours sitting next to Rulon Gardner, the Greco Roman wrestling gold medal winner from the 2000 Olympic games. He was there as a guest speaker, but by the end of those two hours Tracie had Rulon rolling with laughter, and vice versa, and she was introducing him to her husband and family.

Rulon just told them laughingly, "I don't know how you guys do it, living with her." They ended up exchanging email addresses and I'd bet they stayed friends.

Tracie helped clean the car, fetched fuel, made food runs, helped Jan with the lineups, was always there to hand a tool or hold a part, and did whatever else was needed to help out. But I believe her main duty was to keep things lively and stirred up in our pit area.

Tracie's son Shane was a college student at the time and near the end of his school days. He was a tall and athletic kid who had been a soccer star for the teams he played for in high school and college. Happy-go-lucky, outgoing, and possessing an above average sense of humor, Shane evidently got his mouth from his mom.

Early on Shane never let his inexperience get in the way of voicing his opinion on matters related to the sprint car. In fact, you had to be careful what you said around Shane, for it might come back to haunt you later if he had a conversation with Jerry.

Case in point: One time Jerry created a part for his car that he called a "stabilizer." In reality it was what you would call an anti-roll bar, or anti-sway bar, which was illegal as far as the track's rulebook was concerned.

No track official ever said anything about the part though because, frankly, we weren't having any success whatsoever at the time. Anyway, Shane and I discussed this part and came to the conclusion that we really didn't think it was helping. The next thing I know Shane was telling Jerry that in his opinion the part should come off, and that I agreed.

Shane was itching to get behind the wheel of a race car and at one point bought an old junk car and some steel tubing in order to build a stock car. That fell through for some reason and he ended up selling it. Then he bought a 305 cubic inch engine to place in a sprint car, but later put it up for sale. Then he purchased a cage cart, which is basically a go-cart that looks like a little sprint car.

He raced the cage cart at a track south of Knoxville and gained great first-hand experience dealing with break downs and struggling with handling issues. He also experienced his first nasty flip and had to work through what was likely a mild concussion. I do not think a week went by without Shane offering his driving services for Jerry's sprint car.

Tracie did not seem to have any interest whatsoever in encouraging her son's racing aspirations.

Shane was a real go-getter and fast learner, and helped out with all aspects of the car. For a while Shane's buddy Justin Cook helped out also, and the youthful exuberance the duo injected into the team became contagious. I don't know if Jerry mellowed over the years, but I could tell he enjoyed Shane's eagerness and appreciated his help.

There have been a host of others who helped Jerry's racing career. Bob Thompson, better known as Booby, probably helped Jerry more than anyone. A successful 360 driver himself and owner of American Challenge Racing, a company that built sprint car chassis in those days, Bob is a veritable walking encyclopedia of sprint car knowledge.

Somewhat aloof and a man who could say more in a few words than most can say in several sentences, his presence in our pit area was a relief and meant that a solution to a problem was close at hand.

Although I had been with Jerry to Bob's shop several times I don't believe I ever said a word to him, probably because I felt he could see right through me and knew I really didn't know what I was doing. The truth of the matter is he likely didn't know I existed.

A guy who clearly cared about helping people, Booby let Jerry build a car in his shop after Jerry destroyed his original car in a crash at Knoxville. John DeMoss, who worked for Booby at the time, said that was the first time he had ever seen Bob allow someone else's car to be built in his shop. Several years after officially retiring from his racing career, Bob regularly raced a non-winged 305 cubic inch sprint car, and rarely lost any of those races he entered.

It was a Kenny Minor built engine that rested between the frame rails of Jerry's sprint car when he won his first ever A feature at the Iowa State Fair Speedway. Kenny was a big, older gentleman whose reddish bushy sideburns and ever-present hat and pipe made me think we were dealing with an old-time Irishman. Maybe we were for all I know. Kenny was never far from our pit stall at the fairgrounds, ready to dip his hands under the hood if needed.

Later on Jerry went with an Ostrich Racing engine, built by Knoxville Raceway Hall of Famer and former 360 Knoxville Nationals champion, Lee Nelson.

One time while under a rain delay during the 360 Nationals, when they had us pit in the barns, Lee helped me with changing the rear radius rod frame mounting positions on Jerry's car. While changing them he gave me an in-depth explanation about how the different frame mounting positions can affect the birdcage and therefore traction and handling. He wasn't obligated to provide the explanation, but I was much obliged for his willingness to freely pass along his vast knowledge.

I know there were many others who helped Jerry race in many ways over the years. You could say that it takes a village to race a sprint car. However even if he didn't have any help, I believe Jerry would have found a way to do it all on his own.

A Night at the Races

I planned my day around going to the races on race day.
Normally on Saturdays, this meant trying to complete any
chores, like mowing the lawn, before I left for Knoxville in the
afternoon. I kept busy to push the nagging feeling of guilt to
the back of my mind, knowing I would be leaving my kids
behind while I went to have fun later that night.

An oddity, in my case I am the only member of my family
who had any involvement in racing, other than the occasional
attendance at a race. That isn't entirely true since my mom's
maiden name is Kain, and I understand we are distantly related
to Freddie Kain, who fielded cars at Knoxville for years. But as
someone once wrote, "Kains are as thick as sparrows," in these
parts, and I never met or had any association with Freddie's
branch of the family tree.

In many cases racing involvement passes from generation
to generation, but not in mine. When my dad was a young man
running the streets of Runnells he did on occasion spend some
time at a shop that once housed a race car driven by Earl
Wagner, who became Pleasantville's very own National Sprint
Car Hall of Fame inductee. But that is the extent of any
previous family involvement in the sport. I wonder if this is a
case of skipping a generation because my kids showed little
interest in regularly attending the races, so they stayed home.
Probably a smart move on their part.

Since the races don't end until anywhere from 10:00 p.m. to

well after midnight, this activity usually negated any other Saturday night plans. I lost count of the number of weddings, reunions, graduation open houses, or other family activities I missed over the years, because I just had to go to the races.

Sometime in the afternoon I'd clean up from whatever work I'd done around the house and prepare to go to the races. The attire for a pit crew guy at Knoxville can vary greatly from team to team. In my case I dressed in something I didn't care got ruined - a sweatshirt or jacket and jeans in the spring, pared down to t-shirt and shorts through the summer. After Jerry had t-shirts made I'd wear one of those.

I don't know if warmer springtime temperatures following a harsh Iowa winter lures us into not dressing warmer at the beginning of a season or not, but I have never been as cold as I have been at the start of the racing schedule at Knoxville. I believe we're all jealous of the rescue crew snug in their fireproof suits at the beginning of the year, but not so much during the sweltering heat of summer.

I had it a lot easier than many pit crew guys on other teams. Since I lived east of Runnells, 25 minutes from Knoxville, and Jerry lived in Des Moines, more like 45 minutes from Knoxville, I met up with him at the track and missed out on the job of loading the trailer. That process can take some time. Not only does the car need to be loaded, but any spare parts, tools, and supplies. Plus stocking the all-important cooler with snacks, pop, water, and beer. It can be an all-day chore.

At around 4:30 p.m. I'd fill up my trusty water jug and head out for Knoxville. People who don't live in Iowa think the state is flat, but in this area it is not. I enjoyed driving through the rolling hills on County Road F-70 and Highway 14, looking out for deer, turkeys, and any other critters that might run across my path.

It seemed curious to me to see people out doing other things - working in their yards, washing their cars, grilling out, etc. - why weren't they going to the races? Oh, right, they're the normal ones. I'd try to mentally prepare myself a bit along the way, and say a little prayer to keep everyone safe for the night.

Even though I had been there hundreds of times, I got goose bumps every time I drove into Knoxville on race day.

Seeing the racing themed Knoxville welcome sign on the outskirts of the city, and the chassis of a sprint car mounted high on a post in a yard north of the track. The National Sprint Car Hall of Fame & Museum, and the huge grandstand with the line of suites on top. It truly is a site to behold for a sprint car junkie.

This is a town that knows where its bread and butter comes from. An anomaly, this town actually embraces its racetrack, and I hope that continues. As Des Moines stretches its tentacles and more cities become suburbs and bedroom towns, especially with the four-lane road that now leads to Knoxville, I hope people who move there know what they're getting into.

It's a friendly town and welcomes you with open arms, but if you move there you better realize there are going to be a lot of people milling about on Saturday nights in the summer. Also be aware that the population triples in size for a week in August during the Knoxville Nationals and preceding events. And if you didn't know, sprint cars are very loud. So if you move to Knoxville, no bitching about the noise. That would be like moving next to a hog lot and then complaining about the smell.

I turned right at the stoplights at West Larson Street just before the museum and headed west, turned into the back gate of the fairgrounds, and followed the driveway to the grassy area behind turn three of the track. On most regular nights this drive wasn't a problem. However if there was a backup at the sign in windows of the Pit Shack I sometimes had to weave my way through the maze of trucks and trailers waiting to pull into the pits.

Parking really isn't a problem until the Nationals hit town. If Knoxville can be knocked for anything, it's parking during Nationals. For the most part they shut the fairgrounds down so unless you have some special credential, job, disability tag, or some distinct reason to be let in, you basically just have to find a place to park in town.

Not that there is a shortage of enterprising individuals and groups who will rent you a place to park on a lawn, private drive, business parking lot, or local ball field. This will set you back anywhere from $3 to $10. But when I think about it, it really is part of the charm. Kind of like I've heard the parking is around Wrigley Field in Chicago.

The best place I ever parked for Nationals was in a field across the railroad tracks just south and west of the fairgrounds. I had seen aerial photos of the track in the past and noticed cars parked in that field, but there was no access road to the fairgrounds. How did those cars get there? I thought it was a case of where you couldn't get there from here.

I later found out from Jerry that you could gain access to the field from the west side of town. If you came in on Highway 92 from the west and turned off at the first Knoxville exit, you just took a left at the "Greatest Parking Spot on Earth" sign and followed the arrow pointing north. Once on that road you continued a few hundred yards and turned at the next sign pointing east onto a long farm driveway.

You stopped at the farmhouse and paid the fee to the kid standing in the yard, which I think was only about $3. Maybe you bought a soda they were selling out of a cooler as well. Then they pointed you to an open gate in the fence leading to their field.

You followed the little path on the edge of the field of corn or beans (depending on the year). The path went east, then to the north, then back to the east, until it arrived at a several acres spot where they didn't plant anything - saved just for the Nationals. There were usually dozens of cars and even some campers parked in this spot. Looking to the east you realized you were within a couple hundred yards of the grandstand.

After you parked you walked east to the end of the clearing and followed a short trail they had mowed through the weeds, until you reached the railroad tracks at the edge of the farmer's property. You then carefully walked across some railroad ties placed over the ditch, crossed the railroad tracks, walked across more railroad ties over the other ditch, and bam, you were there. This tucked away little area really was the greatest parking spot on earth!

I'd heard that the fair board didn't appreciate this enterprise. One possible reason is there wasn't an entry to the fairgrounds from that direction, and sometimes you had to duck under or hop over a rope on the perimeter of fairground's property. There was probably some kind of safety or liability issue involved. I'm guessing the farmer made more money on the ground he kept cleared for parking than he would have made if crops had been planted in the area.

Unfortunately, the railroad put a stop to my favorite Nationals parking spot I believe due to the fact that people had to walk across the tracks. I think they took notice one year after RAGBRAI, the annual bike ride across Iowa known for its partying, made an overnight stop in Knoxville. It seems an individual made the poor decision to sleep on the railroad tracks and did not fare very well when a train came by that night. He survived, however not long thereafter my favorite Nationals parking spot came to an end.

But on normal nights I would park in the grassy area behind turn three as far away as possible from the track. I did this consciously to protect my car from the normal mud flung over the fence, but also in an effort to avoid any errant wheels or broken sprint car parts which have been known to clear the fence during crashes.

I'd make my way to the Pit Shack located under the west edge of the main grandstand, and walked amongst the trucks and trailers waiting for their occupants to return after signing in. It's there where I would catch the first whiff of diesel fuel emanating from the tow vehicles, which is a smell that will forever bring back memories of Knoxville.

This walk also often produced my first sighting of promoter Ralph Capatani of the evening, patrolling the area in his golf cart, ever-present radio at the ready. Arrivals were sure to receive a welcoming nod from this legendary Hall of Famer if they happened to catch his eye.

Early in the season there was usually a long line to sign in at the Pit Shack. I don't know if it was because they were working the bugs out of the sign in process, or maybe all the pit crew guys didn't have their crew cards, or what, but it could be a 15 to 20 minute wait. It was interesting standing in that line though, because you got to rub shoulders with some of the greatest names in modern day sprint car racing, and see some from days of old.

I got a real kick out of standing in line and listening to all the other crews and drivers talk about other races they'd participated in recently, how they did, what problems they might have experienced, or just the light-hearted crap they slung at each other. There was a real sense of camaraderie.

When the World of Outlaws were in town you saw the greatest sprint car drivers in the world standing in line, just like the rest of us, waiting to obtain their pit passes. The World of Outlaws is the premier sprint car series on earth. Founded in 1978 by Hall of Fame inductee Ted Johnson, this group of racing vagabonds crisscross the country from February to November and compete in 90-plus shows every year.

They go up against the local stars at every track, plus any true "outlaw" professional race teams who don't follow any particular sanctioning body and chase a schedule of their own. Sprint car racing is what they do for a living. Their grueling schedule and work ethic is legendary, and their lifestyles are fascinating.

Traveling border to border and coast to coast, rock bands, triple-A baseball teams, and politicians on the verge of elections have nothing on the World of Outlaws when it comes to their schedule. Sometimes competing in multiple races at multiple tracks hours apart in a week's time, the logistics alone are mind-boggling. Let alone keeping the car maintained, restocking supplies, eating something besides racetrack food, and trying to find a few hours to sleep now and then.

They even bring a crew of officials of their own who work with the locals to run the race program, set up and tear down promotional displays, and deal with sketchy internet and communications networks. They're racing's version of a traveling circus, except with a much cooler high-speed form of entertainment to promote.

The cost to keep these teams on the road all year long is astounding. Professional race teams in particular (and all racers in general) tend to be proud and unabashed solicitors when it comes to funding their racing operations – and more power to them. They'll do whatever it takes to get to the racetrack, and it's refreshing to see there isn't a hint of an effort to make you think otherwise. I'm willing to bet that if a large feminine hygiene company offered up 500 grand to run a year with the Outlaws, someone would be driving a pink car with the company's name plastered all over the side, and they'd be happy to hand out free samples after the races every night.

I've sometimes felt that grassroots team crewmembers at Knoxville are a bit spoiled and lead somewhat of a Forrest Gump life while being around this kind of environment – meaning they often just kind of fall into awesome experiences. It's a unique feeling to be mowing your lawn out in the country east of Runnells on a Saturday afternoon, and then just a few short hours later walk into the pits at Knoxville and glance over to see someone like Tony Stewart leaning up against a trailer.

I also believe that simply being a sprint car fan (which we all are) makes it harder to be impressed by other things in life.

For example you might go to a concert or something and afterwards think, "That was cool, but it wasn't witnessing-Bobby-Allen-win-the-1990-Knoxville-Nationals cool."

Once I reached the Pit Shack window I showed my crew card, paid the $15 pit crew admission (it was $5 when Jerry started in 1991), signed the release form, and received my wristband. For some reason I saved most, if not all, of the tickets and pit passes I purchased over the years.

I do not know why I have kept these things. I have a 2-gallon glass jar full of them at home. Do I think someone would actually be interested in seeing them some day? Do I think I'll go through and total the amount of money I've spent over the years at some point? I don't plan on doing that because I believe it would make me sick to my stomach. I guess it was just habit.

If I was lucky I timed my arrival with that of Jerry's and rode into the pits in his motor home. If not I walked through the pit gate and crossed the track by foot to reach the pits. This can be an eventful walk if the water truck has recently passed by the pit gate. As tacky as the surface can be early in a night of racing, or as hard and abrasive it can be after the races, when it is wet it can be nearly as slippery as wet ice.

During the 1987 Nationals, the year it rained three of the four days of the event, it became a spectator sport to watch people slip and fall trying to walk across the wet track. I have a videotape of the *Sports Cavalcade* broadcast of that year's Nationals which shows footage of a few people falling or nearly falling on their behinds trying to walk across the slippery track. It was awfully entertaining and the crowd roared their approval for falls and amusing saves.

It happened again during a rain delay at the 2005 Nationals, and some of the loudest cheers of the week occurred when several unfortunate souls failed to cross the track entirely on their feet.

My goal when crossing the track was to not provide anyone with any entertainment whatsoever. Other than some close calls, I was successful.

After Jerry parked his rig in a pit stall (which was usually a process of a track official telling him to park in one spot and Jerry parking where he wanted, old-school Jerry once again) we unloaded the car, jack, tires, and other assorted items from the trailer and set up shop for the night.

Sprint car tow vehicles and trailers vary greatly. On one end of the spectrum they can simply be a pickup truck, with tools and parts thrown in the bed, pulling an open trailer. On the other end they can consist of semis pulling enclosed trailers, stocked with an inventory of parts and a spare car or two, and lack nothing when compared to NASCAR or IndyCar trailers.

Jerry's first trailer was enclosed, but small enough to necessitate the removal of the sprint car's top wing and modification of the trailer's wheel wells in order to squeeze the car inside. It also had two doors that opened to the sides, rather than a drop ramp door, and required two ramps to line up so we could push the car through the door opening.

His next trailer was much larger and he pulled it with a motor home he had acquired. It had white interior walls, a work bench, and a place for his tool box to be strapped down. It was well-lit from electricity powered by a gas generator (which could be a cantankerous s.o.b. sometimes), and wheels were stored on short posts Jerry mounted perpendicular to the side of one wall. He also built racks which held a multitude of torsion bars, radius rods, and rear end gears.

The back of the roof was raised more than enough to accommodate the top wing, and the top would have made a great vantage point to stand on and view the races. But doing so is a big no-no in the pits at Knoxville, as it hinders the view of the fans in the stands. You're reminded of this rule religiously by the infield announcer whenever someone commits an infraction.

Toward the end of his career Jerry went with a basic open trailer, which went along just fine with his old-school persona.

Trailers can become jealous of all the mechanical care and money lavished on the race car, and sometimes they act out in order to gain some attention of their own. We found that out late one Sunday night coming home from a race in Moberly, Missouri. A problem with the hitch forced Jerry to leave the trailer on the side of the road and come back to deal with later. We got to Des Moines just in the nick of time for me to call in sick for work before my shift started that Monday morning.

For a period of time I believe Robert Bell, known as "The Colfax Comet," should have been presented with a "Most Unique Race Car Trailer" award, due to the imaginative creation he conceived to haul his car and equipment. It consisted of a large fifth-wheel camper trailer he had gutted and then installed a large drop ramp door at the back.

When Robert raced at Knoxville he was a regular visitor to our pit stall, and his parents stopped by for a chat with Jerry after the races nearly every race night. Robert occasionally purchased parts from Jerry, and I suspect those parts were well-used by the time we got done with them.

One of the funniest quotes I ever heard came from Robert Bell. One night Jerry asked him why he pulled into the pits after a red flag during a B feature Robert had competed in.

Robert replied, "That's where the push truck pushed me!"

I was happy to see the reaction Robert received after winning a heat race at the 2017 Chili Bowl Nationals midget races.

No one on earth loves racing more than Robert Bell.

If someone had taken an inventory of the things I carried in my pockets at different times throughout the night, they might have found a flathead screwdriver, 9/16th inch wrench, ¾ inch wrench, and a tire tape.

The flathead screwdriver (the one with the wide head, just the right size to fit in my back pocket – I was very protective of it) was used for the multitude of dzus buttons attached all over the car. Dzus buttons were used mainly to hold the hood and side panels on, but also for wheel covers and other areas.

A dzus button is an ingenious fastener that is inserted through the hole of one panel, continues through the hole of another panel or tab, and snaps on to a little spring riveted across the hole on the other side of the second panel or tab. It only took a quarter turn to attach a dzus button, and it was a quick and reliable fastener. Jerry had a tool box drawer full of these fasteners and I'm not sure I'd like to know how much time I spent searching that drawer for the exact size dzus button I needed.

I realize some of this has changed since then, but at the time the $9/16^{th}$ and $\frac{3}{4}$ inch wrenches came in handy because those sized nuts and bolts were common on a sprint car. The $9/16^{th}$ could be used on torsion stops, torsion bars, steering arm, rear end cover, parts of the wing mounting structure, and other areas I'm forgetting. The $\frac{3}{4}$ could be used on radius rods and shocks. A person could have completed a fair amount of sprint car assembly or disassembly with those two size wrenches. Besides that, a wrench sticking out of your back pocket made you look like a mechanic, at least at first glance.

The tire tape is a small and thin tape measure used to measure tire stagger. To measure stagger you hook the end of the tape on a tire tread of the larger tire, roll the tire on the ground or spin it on the axle, and make note of the number of inches of circumference.

You then do the same with the smaller tire, but keep feeding the tape once you go past its circumference, and stop and put your thumb at the number you made note of when you measured the larger tire (and if you already forgot that number, which does happen, you start the process over). The overlapped part of the tape tells you the exact difference in circumference between the two tires, so, voilà! No math!

I may have "forgotten" to take a tire tape out of my pocket after the last race Jerry ever ran. It may be orange, have a JOCKOS Sprint Parts sticker on the side, and reside on a shelf in my man cave. Just in case Jerry had been looking for it. But I count that tire tape as my career earnings from sprint car racing.

Although a real mechanic I do not claim to be, there was a process I went through at the beginning of the night. For one,

I went around and checked the tightness of every radius rod, torsion arm, torsion stop, steering arm, wing mount, and any other nut and bolt I could find.

Some observed this and made comments such as, "Don't you trust Jerry?" Of course I did, but the scary thing is I did occasionally find loose nuts. My greatest fear was something falling off the car. That would have been bad. So I guess you could say I was rather obsessed, or maybe anal would be a better word, with making sure nuts and bolts were tight.

This obsession had caused some problems in the past. On one occasion at the Iowa State Fairgrounds, early in Jerry's career, I was checking the tightness of the lug nuts on his car's left front wheel. Jerry had a lug nut wrench which was a long extension shaped in a Y. On the one end was a socket, and at the other end were two handles.

I was really cranking on that wrench, putting my weight into it, when, snap, a lug broke off. At the time I didn't realize the lugs were made of aluminum. Jerry educated me after I brought what I had done to his attention.

This wouldn't have been a huge problem except that, a) by design there were only a total of three lug nuts that held the wheel on in the first place, b) they had just called for sprint cars to line up for the feature, and, c) our pit stall was right next to Bob Trostle's, and I was embarrassed that this legendary figure might have seen me do this stupid thing.

"Dammit, Todd, you tighten the shit out of everything. You need to develop a feel for it," was all Jerry had to say.

We didn't have a spare lug bolt, or even the time to replace the broken one if we had. The pattern for the three lugs was a triangle. In between those were some unused holes in the wheel which led to threads in the hub. We didn't have a bolt with the correct threads to fit one of those so Jerry went to Bob Thompson's trailer and borrowed one, and then screwed it into one of the unused holes.

To say that it was Jerry-rigged (pun intended) would be appropriate. It just didn't look right. I didn't like it one bit, especially since it was my fault.

"It'll be all right, let's go," Jerry said as he climbed into the cockpit and strapped in.

I don't think I have ever been as nervous for the start of a race as I was for that one. All that ran through my mind were visions of that left front wheel falling off the car as it entered turn one and Jerry experiencing a series of vicious flips.

But immediately after they threw the green flag Jerry pulled into the pits. I expected him to come out of the cockpit unhappy with me because the wheel was wobbling or something, but in reality the engine had lost oil pressure. That was the happiest I had ever been after seeing him drop out of a race.

I also experienced problems with the rear wheel nuts. For the rear there is just one big nut for each wheel. They both tighten towards the back of the car, therefore the right side one has reverse threads (which can cause confusion early in the season, or if you're trying to change that wheel in a hurry during a red flag). This is because when the driver is on the throttle the rear axle is spinning forward, so if anything the axle is trying to tighten the nut itself, since the nut tightens towards the back.

Anyway, back to my obsession, I did not feel right unless I checked the tightness of these nuts at least three times before each time the car hit the track. It was like a nervous twitch or something – I just had to do it. Even if I had just checked them 10 minutes ago, if any thought at all crossed my mind that I hadn't checked them, I had to recheck them.

For a while Jerry had a wheel wrench that was shaped in a T and was sometimes called a wheel nut whacker. At one end was the big socket, and at the other end was a bar that attached perpendicular to the shaft. There were circular heavy pieces of metal connected to both ends of the bar, and the bar could rotate almost 180 degrees on the shaft. So when you had the socket on the nut and rotated the bar at the other end you hammered the nut on or off, depending on which direction you were rotating the bar.

I had a difficult time developing a "feel" for that tool, so usually I'd just hammer away until Jerry yelled, "That's enough!" Again, I really didn't want the wheel falling off the car.

One night he must not have caught me in time and I apparently really tightened the nut. I'm not sure if it was totally my fault, or the axle tightened the nut itself, or what, but that thing simply would not come off. We tried other types of wheel wrenches, standing on it, bigger and stronger people trying – no matter what we did that stupid nut would not come off. Jerry ended up having to cut the nut off the axle with an air chisel back at his shop.

The next week he brought a different type of wheel wrench, which we used to the end. It was in the shape of a tall L, with the socket on the short end and the long handle perpendicular to the socket. It was better to get a feel for this tool, but I had to use some trial and error. I found if I tightened using one arm, blocking the tire with my leg and pulling the wrench handle towards me, I could usually loosen it using both arms.

We still had trouble sometimes and it was not uncommon to see one of us standing and bouncing on the wrench handle to loosen a nut. At least we never had a part fall off the car. I'm pretty sure Jerry still thought I "tightened the shit" out of everything.

Manually pushing sprint cars all over the infield is one task crewmembers don't need to be concerned with at Knoxville. This is because the track spoils you with an army of push trucks and 4-wheelers, whose job it is to move cars to the staging area and anywhere else they need to be during the night (in addition to the push trucks packing the track and starting the cars).

They save crews a lot of manual labor and probably don't receive the credit they deserve for keeping the show running on time. At Knoxville you can back your car out of your pit stall and it seems a 4-wheeler or push truck materializes out of nowhere to push it wherever it needs to go. I've been to tracks where this isn't the case, and push vehicles have a definite impact on the racing program. You need to keep an eye out for them though, as they're usually hustling through the pits because they have places to go and people to see.

The push truck guys and gals seem to have their own subset of the sprint car subculture. While they receive a small stipend, which hopefully covers the gas they burn, they spend countless hours and drive many miles around the track and through the infield every year.

Like everything else in sprint car racing, the quality of push trucks can vary greatly. You see some that appear to have just come off the showroom floor, all the way down to the poor guy who is seemingly under his truck every week wiring up the exhaust that just won't stay put. The amount of mud they scrape off their vehicles every year could likely build a second racetrack somewhere.

The Iowa State Fairgrounds was one of those places that didn't seem to have enough push trucks sometimes. If you were pitted on the south end of the pits, that push up the gradual hill to the track entrance on turn two kind of sucked. Pushing with your head down, occasionally looking around in a futile hope that a push truck might magically appear. Cursing the stagger that seemed to be laughing at and intentionally working against you as you pushed. Glancing at the stock cars with a tinge of jealousy of their self-starting systems.

Of course all of that went away when the green flag dropped, because sprint cars kick ass.

Pit crew duties vary throughout the night, but a couple routine ones involve fueling the car and dealing with issues related to mud.

Fueling a sprint car is an easy and common thing to do. You simply pop the cap off the tank, insert the funnel, and pour in methanol from a 5-gallon jug. The only things we needed to be concerned with was if Smooth had a lit cigarette, and if your face became too close to the funnel you discovered that fumes from methanol fuel do a great job of clearing your sinuses and watering your eyes.

Being able to tell how much fuel the tank held was sometimes a different story. You didn't want more fuel than necessary because liquid is heavy. If the level was above the ledge in the tank you could see it with a flashlight, peering through the opening, death grip on the flashlight so as not to drop it in the tank. If the level was below the ledge it was a little more difficult. Jerry had a wooden dipstick with notches cut into it representing gallons, which we could insert into the tank. Methanol evaporates fast, so you had to look at the stick quickly after pulling it from the tank.

If I was near when the officials who acted as the track fuel testers came along I would cheerfully pop the fuel cap off the tank to allow them access to obtain a sample. Even though we never dabbled with fuel tampering, these two officials made me nervous. They were the nicest couple, but they gave me the same feeling as when a police officer pulls me over as a courtesy just to advise my tags are about to expire.

Speaking of track officials, that's another group of people who likely don't receive the credit they deserve. I don't know the conditions of their employment, but would be hard-pressed to believe it is worth the time commitment and grief they sometimes take. It has to be difficult because they can't show any partiality whatsoever to drivers or teams. And it's not often that drivers, car owners, or crewmembers seek out an official to tell them how great everything is going. They have to love it, because some of them have been around forever. Track officials must all be true race fans.

Making runs to the fuel truck to fill empty fuel jugs was a regular nightly chore, and once filled it was easier to carry two of the 5-gallon jugs rather than awkwardly carry one. After arriving at the fuel truck you got in line, loosened the jug caps to save time, and waited your turn.

When your turn came up the fueler simply asked, "Who's it for?" I'd say, "Crabb 12x," and they'd fill the jugs and hand over a receipt. It was heartening to see their trust in the process. Tracie completed this duty often and was able to carry the heavy jugs effortlessly, because she's a badass.

Another consideration regarding fuel was the size of the fuel pill to use. I suppose it was called a pill since it's a little larger than an aspirin, but you wouldn't want to swallow one because they were made of brass. The number printed on one side identified the size of the hole drilled through the middle, and the smaller the hole meant the richer the pill.

To change one you simply uncoupled the bypass relief valve located in the cockpit near the gear slider, and swapped out the old one. The bypass is used to route unused fuel back to the tank, and that's why the smaller the pill equals less excess fuel going to the tank equals more flowing to the engine.

While uncoupling the valve care had to be taken to not allow the spring or existing pill to pop out uncontrollably. Otherwise you and anyone nearby would be on hands and knees searching the floor pan or surrounding dirt for the errant pill and/or spring. You also had to make sure the correct pill was selected, which wasn't easy because the numbers were tiny and difficult to read. Jerry kept a magnifying glass handy just for this purpose. You also needed to make sure the pill was inserted in the right direction, as one side of the hole was beveled more than the other.

Jerry got around the task of swapping out pills for a time by using a dial-a-jet device. Several different sizes of pills could be inserted into the mechanism, and to change the size of the pill you simply turned the dial. It also virtually eliminated the need for us to search for a pill or spring that went rogue.

Mechanical fuel injection adjustments are important and can depend greatly on the weather. Early in the year or late in the fall, when the air was cool and low in humidity, you could run the engines richer and feed those beasts.

Also related is the number of times you see someone standing directly behind an idling car in the pits, with furrowed brows in deep concentration. They may be doing this because it's cool to hear that crisp, sweet sound, but they're probably trying to tell if the sound they're hearing is balanced between the two sides of the engine. If it isn't it could indicate a fuel or some other issue.

Sometimes you see guys licking their fingers and quickly touching the header near each exhaust port. They're not doing this because they're masochists – they're really trying to determine if one is markedly cooler than the others, which would also indicate a problem. Jerry reduced the chance of burned fingers once he purchased a heat-sensor gun.

Scraping mud off the car is more important than it sounds because mud is fairly dense and heavy, especially early in the night. It may sound mundane, and it probably is, but I found it interesting.

It was remarkable to discover the areas on the car where mud accumulated. There were the obvious places, like the front and underside of wings, side panels, and wheel covers. But mud in the not so obvious spots - like the front of the bottom of the fuel tank, the inside of a wheel rim, behind the seat, on top of and below the floor pan, on the motor plate, and other nooks and crannies - made me wonder how the hell that mud got there. It was as if someone took the car and had it powder-coated with black zook clay.

These hard to reach places did train you on where to spray Mudd-Off prior to the car entering the track. Mudd-Off is a magical slippery liquid which eases the removal of mud. I know it does because of the difficult time we had with mud removal the few times we forgot to spray down the car or had ran out of the liquid.

Dirt clods kicked up on the track during a race can be ginormous, have been known to cause damage, and can become dangerous.

I recall one race when Jerry pulled in early, which seemed odd because the car appeared to be performing well. Once at our pit stall we found the rock guard, which is a cage-like structure attached to the front of the roll cage to protect the driver, seemed to be missing. This is because a large clod had pushed the guard inside the cage, the guard now rested across Jerry's arms, and prevented him from steering effectively. Apparently the clod disintegrated because the cockpit floor was full of small dirt clods.

Helmet shield tear-offs are another important product designed to solve the problems caused by other cars blasting mud at a driver's face. They are simply thin, clear strips of plastic layered over the shield. When one becomes muddied the driver reaches up, tears it off, and the next one in line takes over mud blocking duties.

I never installed these on Jerry's helmet, but sometimes it seemed they could be tricky. The pull tabs had to be folded over in just such a way so that only the top one could be grasped when it needed to be removed. I have a lot of memories of Jan installing these, counting the number of folded tabs, and smoothing the surface with her shirttail in order to squeeze out any air bubbles between the strips of plastic.

I've seen instances where drivers went to pull a tear-off and inadvertently pulled them all off at once. When that occurs they have to go old school and try to keep their shields clear with their hand. This could mean simply wiping the shield off with their glove, which can cause a big-time smear. But sometimes they hold their hand in front of them almost as if they're trying to block the sun from their eyes (which they also do), but in this case they're blocking the mud.

I'm always impressed with how drivers may be coming out of a corner, in traffic at full throttle, and have the wherewithal to reach up and remove a tear-off. I suppose it's something they learn quickly, as it seems it would be difficult driving on rough dirt tracks at 100+ M.P.H. while blinded by mud.

For a time you saw a few drivers use an automated device to keep their shields clear. Twedt had one and it consisted of a roll of the clear plastic encased on one side of the helmet, the plastic stretched across the shield, and spooled to an encasement on the other side of the helmet.

When the shield became muddied the driver simply pressed a button, which activated the electric motor on the spooling side of the helmet, and it pulled clear plastic from the other side. These devices worked great, until they didn't. You could easily tell when one malfunctioned due to the forty foot streamer of plastic trailing the car, still attached to the driver's head.

Sometimes mud prevention apparatus can be dangerous. One time Jerry fashioned a screen to protect the front of his radiator. It resembled woven steel, but it really wasn't woven. It reminded me of the steel seats in chairs I've seen, and that could have been its origin. Jerry used a band saw to cut the screen to size and installed it in front of the radiator.

On a night at the races not long after it was installed, I reached under the nose of the car to clean off the mud which had stuck to the screen. What I pulled back was a handful of mud mixed with my own blood. This is because the band saw had created razor sharp pointy edges at each weave all along the sides of the screen, and they did a good job cutting my hand. Earl got on Jerry's case a little bit about how there should never be sharp edges on a race car, and I earned my first duct tape bandages.

At some point Jerry started bringing a bucket of soapy water and sponges to wash the car after mud was removed. I don't know where he got the idea, and no way would I claim we were the first to do it, but I don't recall seeing others do this prior to us. It was a good thing to do - not only because it made the car look nice, but it also gave us a chance to remove the grime and inspect the car for issues up close.

Throughout a normal night we went through these routines, joked and gave each other grief, watched the races, and discussed setup changes while waiting for our next chance to race.

When I say "discussed setup changes" I really mean "listened to whatever changes Jerry wanted to make" and then made those changes. He did ask me what I thought sometimes, but I usually answered his question with a question.

For example if he asked, "What do you think?" I might have answered, "Did the car take off okay?" or "Did the car feel tight or loose?" I was hesitant to offer an opinion, frankly, because everything I knew I had learned from him. So what could I offer that he didn't already know? So basically I bounced questions back at him.

In general adjustments were made to tighten up the car throughout the night as the track went from heavy and tacky to dry and slick (but not always). A tight car makes it feel like it doesn't want to turn, and a loose car feels like the back end is going to come around and cause a spin out. As the track dries out it naturally loses traction, therefore the car normally needs to be "tightened up" as you progress through heat race, B feature, and if you're lucky, A feature.

A dirt track changing in such a way is one of the unique characteristics of dirt track racing. Racers like to see at least two good lines to run on - with one on the bottom, slick in the middle, and one on the top with a nice cushion to lean on.

The cushion is the berm created as cars throw dirt up the track throughout the night. It starts low and gradually moves up the track, and sometimes gets to where it is right up against the fence. It can be nice and even and smooth, all the way to choppy and treacherous. Twedt sometimes raced above the cushion, and described the experience as similar to driving through a plowed field.

A good two lane track was common at Knoxville due to the world-famous track preparation abilities of the Duncan family, who have handled those duties there for years. I only remember the rare occasion where the track took rubber and caused a sticky one-lane single-file no-passing freight train of cars around the bottom. When that happens it makes the crews of the cars at the tail of the field curse under their breath and kick a nearby dirt clod.

These adjustments to tighten the car generally meant lowering tire air pressure, reducing the amount of stagger (which could also involve mounting, siping, and/or grooving a tire), moving the right rear wheel in, taking a turn out of a torsion bar (and rare cases of changing bars), installing a tie-down shock somewhere, changing rear end gears, and/or changing the top wing position. Sprint car adjustments can vary greatly and seem infinite, but these are some of the common ones.

You normally wouldn't make all of these adjustments in a night as it's possible to "dial yourself out of the park," both figuratively and literally. That means you went too far in the direction you wanted to go. There is a line that can be crossed, causing a condition known as tight-loose. When that happens the car is tight going into a corner, has to be forcibly turned more, and then becomes loose - which deceptively makes the driver think the car is loose. Teams can make some of the adjustments for different reasons. Volumes could be written on the different theories regarding sprint car setups.

Lowering tire air pressure puts more of the tire surface on the track, therefore should increase traction. The lowest pressure I remember we ever ran in the right rear tire was 6 lbs., which is pretty low. For a time Jerry ran 13 lbs. in his front tires, and I always thought that was a bit unusual since racers can be notoriously superstitious. For example, none of us wanted anything to do with green M&M's. The color green is a well-known unlucky color in racing. It's considered bad juju. But don't tell Steve Kinser that, since he kicked all kinds of ass while driving a green Quaker State car.

As noted previously, stagger helps the car turn in the corners. Therefore less stagger doesn't help it turn as much, so reducing it tightens up the car. If you already had tires mounted which calculated to the stagger you were looking for, you simply placed those on the car.

If not, you then had to mount a different tire on a rim, which was more of a process. You first took the wheel with the old tire and used the valve stem core removal tool to remove the core and let the air out of the tire. I have seen Jerry loosen some of the bolts holding the bead lock to the wheel in order to speed up air removal, but I'm not sure doing so could be called a recommended method.

Once air had been let out the wheel was placed on its side and you wrestled with the awkward tire bead-breaking tool to break the bead on the side opposite the bead lock, which sometimes seemed to have become one with the wheel.

I believe the bead-breaking tool we used was originally a medieval torture device which was brought forward to current times in order to torment sprint car pit crew guys.

It consisted of a two-handled implement which resembled and acted like a tree pruning shear in reverse. Hinged near the jaws was a bar, and at the other end of the bar was a hook. That hook was placed on the edge of the rim and held there with your foot. You then pushed down on and spread the handles of the tree pruning shear-like tool on the other side of the rim in an effort to create a wedge between the tire and the rim, working yourself around the wheel. After getting a good sweat going and using every curse word in your vocabulary, and learning some new ones from others who tagged in on the bead-breaking wrestling match, you eventually gained victory over the bead.

The wheel was then flipped over and you loosened the one thousand bolts that attach the bead lock to the wheel, which holds that side of the tire to the rim. Once the bead lock was removed you carefully placed it somewhere so the one thousand bolts stayed in the holes, otherwise you might have to play a game of one thousand bolts pick-up (there really wasn't one thousand bolts, it only seemed like it until Jerry brought along an electric impact wrench). You were then able to pull the old tire off the rim.

You then placed the new tire on the rim, attached the bead lock and screwed the one thousand bolts back in, and aired up the tire. If the side opposite of the bead lock (that side you know you're eventually going to have to wrestle again at some point) didn't seat properly you sprayed some soapy water or other lubricant on the rim to help it seat.

Watching that side and waiting for the bead to seat, as air pressure continued to build, made you feel a little like the bomb disposal guy in *The Hurt Locker*. That probably isn't funny because people have been seriously injured and worse from exploding tires while trying to mount them on wheels. There was no mistaking when the bead properly seated, as the report it gave off once seated never failed to startle the bejesus out of me.

Sometimes you might have to sipe or groove a tire. A crewmember or driver siping or grooving a tire is one of the most common sights you see as you stroll through the pits at a sprint car race.

Legend has it that a guy named John Sipe invented siping when he used a razor blade to cut slits in the soles of his shoes in order to gain traction. I don't know if that is true or not but it makes sense, since doing the same thing to a rear sprint car tire has a similar effect. The razor thin slits create more edges and simultaneously aids the tire in heating up and dissipating heat faster, and helps to prevent the tire from blistering.

Grooving appears more drastic as it cuts rubber strips out of the tire. It also creates more edges and helps the tire clean better, especially on heavy tacky tracks. You can easily tell if someone has grooved a tire recently due to the pile of little rubber strips on the ground.

Our siping/grooving tool could be plugged in to heat up in order to cut through the tire more easily. If you didn't have access to electricity you simply cussed throughout the process of doing the job cold (the propensity to curse seems to have a direct correlation to the proximity of the pits at a racetrack). Both siping and grooving was done with the same tool. You used the two open-ended razor blades on the business end of the tool to sipe, and flipped the razor over to the closed side to groove.

If the wheel was on the axle and the car on the ground it could be a one-man job. You simply had to roll the car forward or backward as you advanced around the tire. Otherwise if the car was jacked up it became a two-man job, with one man running the tool and the other holding the tire to keep it from spinning.

It was easier to work your way around the tire if the car was jacked up. The problem with the two-man method was that the one running the tool had to listen to the mocking of his sipping/grooving abilities by the one holding the tire. But if you can't handle being mocked, or can't dish out mocking in return, you probably shouldn't be on a sprint car pit crew.

You see teams create a variety of interesting and creative designs when siping and grooving tires. I just tried to pattern the imaginary line Jerry drew on the tire with his finger. We normally only siped or grooved a tire once it started to become worn. Some of the well-funded teams can regularly be seen siping and grooving a brand spanking new tire. Seeing that always came as somewhat of a shock to those of us who rarely laid hands on a brand new tire.

One thing that can't be denied is the importance of tires, since those are the only four places where a sprint car makes contact with the track. Unless of course something bad has happened.

Moving the right rear wheel in by inserting a smaller wheel spacer between the birdcage and the wheel, or using wheels with more offset, has the effect of putting more weight on that wheel and therefore should cause more traction.

Picture standing sideways on a steep hill. If you have your feet close together, the weight isn't distributed over a wide area, your foot on the downhill side won't slide, and you'll likely tip over. If you widen your stance, the weight distribution is spread out, and you'll probably slide down the hill. That's basically the same thing that happens when moving the right rear wheel in or out.

One thing to keep in mind is not moving the wheel in so far that the tire makes contact with the radius rod. Radius rods are installed with this possibility in mind however, and one end has reverse threads. If installed correctly and a tire happens to rub it a bit, the tire would try to rotate the rod and tighten it on the rod ends, rather than loosen. You still want a space between the tire and radius rod.

If there's a notch in the rod end jam nut it indicates it has reverse threads. I've looked at cars to try and spot one on an end where it isn't supposed to be, which would indicate a rookie mistake, but haven't found one yet.

Taking a turn or so out of a torsion bar has the effect of lowering that corner, which distributes more weight to that area, and therefore should cause more traction in that spot. Putting a turn or so into the opposite corner can do the same thing. Adjusting the torsion bar is only a process of loosening the lock nut and turning the adjuster bolt on the torsion stop on the side opposite the arm you want to change.

I only recall a few instances where we changed torsion bars at the track. With two at the front and two at the back, they were the spring of choice for the suspension on most sprint cars - although some dabbled in coil-over shock springs. Spring rates for torsion bars depend on their thickness, and the spring part comes from the resistance to twisting the bar. I only realized they could be utilized on passenger vehicles when I spent a day replacing one that had broken on a 1995 Chevy Astro van I once owned.

In general a softer bar generated more traction since that corner sagged more, distributed more weight there, and helped on dry-slick tracks. Stiffer bars wouldn't sag the corner as much, didn't distribute as much weight, therefore caused less traction and was better for heavy tacky tracks. Setting the ride height was done by adjusting the torsion bars, and Jerry would do this by blocking the car.

He would start by picking his choice of several wooden blocks he had cut to size. The block was placed on the top of the bottom bar of the frame just below the axle. The frame was then jacked up until the block met the bottom of the axle. The torsion stop was then adjusted until the torsion arm met the top of the front axle, or the resistance felt for the rear torsion arm since it's attached to the bird cage.

You did this on all four corners and the car was blocked. It's a little confusing, because the higher the number of inches the car is blocked, the lower the ride height. Whenever you see a race stoppage for debris on the track due to an errant setup block, it's probably because someone forgot to remove it from the frame after blocking the car. Some guys didn't even mess with blocking. They simply took measurements from the ends of the torsion bars to the ground.

Installing a tie-down shock, which has a slower rebound after compression, kind of does the same thing as lowering that corner (versus an easy-up shock which rebounds faster and compresses slower). Changing a shock was just a two ¾ inch nut job (at the time). I always knew when Jerry wanted a shock changed, as he would wordlessly place one on the tire next to the shock he wanted changed, and then walk away.

I always had a sneaky suspicion that the success top teams experienced had a lot to do with the witchcraft involved in figuring out the innumerable combinations of torsion bars and shocks.

Changing gears was not as complicated as it sounds. Sprint cars utilize a "quick-change" rear end, which is a bit of a misnomer. While not as quick as using a gear shift in a passenger car, it was quicker than, well, I'm not sure what it was quicker than. I suppose quicker than whatever came before it.

I never mastered the nuances regarding which gear ratio was the correct one to run, which can change greatly depending on the size of the track and track conditions. In general sometimes a higher gear was installed when the track slicked off. It's kind of based on the same principle as why you don't stomp on the gas in your passenger car on icy roads. I just made sure I got the gears I was told to install, that they were installed with the numbers on the gears facing out (for some reason), and that the big gear went on top. That was important or otherwise you could end up with a gear ratio more suited for the Indy 500.

To change the gears you first placed the catch pan under the rear end and then removed the $9/16^{th}$ inch nuts from the rear end cover. You pulled the cover off and, if the car recently came off the track, played a game of "hot potato" with the steaming hot gears after you pulled them out. This wasn't bad if you remembered to grab the leather glove or a towel to protect your hand.

You then inserted the new gears, wiggling them a little to align the outside teeth on each gear along with the splines that go through the insides. On our rear end you next played a game of reverse "Operation" to carefully find just the right angle and alignment to slide the cover back on, replaced the nuts, and poured the rear end grease back in.

I've watched crew guys lying on the ground, maybe sort of on a mat, wallowing around while changing gears. I found it easier to jack the frame up slightly to lift the bottom of the fuel tank out of the way, and simply kneeled down and reached under to change gears. My clothes got filthy enough during a night of racing without rolling around in the dirt.

The wing acts as an upside down plane airfoil, and increasing the angle increases down force overall. Moving the wing towards the back obviously increases down force on the rear tires. However too much wing angle creates too much drag, since that wing can also act like a sail.

Moving the wing too far back can cause wheelies, which is damn cool to witness, but makes steering difficult for the driver. I saw Danny Young win a wheelie contest once after lowering the rear end and moving the wing all the way back. I believe he won because the wheelie was so high it caused the rear bumper to tear off after it dug into the dirt.

When Jerry first started racing at Knoxville the 360 class was required to use 16 square foot top wings, I guess as a way to save wear and tear on engines since it takes some oomph to pull those sails. For a while teams in the 360 class came up with imaginative wings which were tilted to the right and shaped somewhat like a parallelogram.

I liked it better when they went to the 25 square foot wings the 410 class used, because it made the 360's look more like sprint cars. It also helped lower costs as the 360's could purchase hand-me-down wings from the 410's, if there was anything left of them.

I have a lot of memories of Jerry holding the mechanical angle finder device to the bottom of the top wing left side panel, tapping the side of the instrument with his finger to make sure the needle wasn't stuck. When he first started racing the 360 class didn't allow the use of the hydraulic mechanism which lets the driver adjust the wing from the cockpit.

Once that ingenious device was allowed it increased exponentially the number of times a driver looks up at the bottom of the wing while circling the track under caution. They do this because they usually mark the bottom of the wing to indicate its starting position, and they want to see how far it has moved since they started jacking around with the slider.

Whenever I saw a noticeable difference in wing angle or position between Jerry's car and other cars with him on the track, a little "uh oh" thought would crop up in the back of my mind. Wings are also useful to test the hardness of your head, which seems to inadvertently happen multiple times throughout a season.

The craziest wing (and car) design I ever saw belonged to a Texas engineer named Tom Johnson, who, as legend has it, designed his car using a CAD program. I saw him race it at the Knoxville Nationals once and if I remember correctly it went through the corners like a mother, but was a tad squirrelly on the straights.

I can't even begin to describe that thing. Google "Tom Johnson sprint car," click on "Images" and "Video," and take a look.

During most nights at Knoxville I would wait with Jerry in the staging area near turn one prior to him being pushed off for his next race. I did this in case he wanted to make any last-minute minor changes, like air pressure or wing adjustment, and to insert the left rear wheel bleeder valve at the last second before he was pushed off.

This was normal practice in an effort to prevent air from escaping unintentionally prior to entering the track. Bleeder valves are used in an attempt to maintain consistent air pressure and "bleed-off" any extra that is created as tires heat up during a race. But if the valve was stuck open, not set exactly right, or set a little below the air pressure you wanted to maintain, you didn't want to insert it until necessary or you might end up with a self-inflicted low tire.

Jerry oftentimes used the "spit bubble" method to set his bleeder valves. This means that once air pressure was set to his liking he would insert the valve, open it enough to allow air to slowly escape, slop some spit on his finger and cover the opening of the valve with it, adjust the valve until it would barely form a spit bubble, then tighten the lock nut. He would then remove the bleeder, wipe off the excess spit on his uniform, and hand it to me. Shane and Justin went back and forth between being disgusted and fascinated by the remarkable consistency of Jerry's spit. (It was clear – not foamy. Resembled baby oil, but more elastic. Weird stuff.)

I'd place the left rear one in my left pocket and right rear one in my right pocket - and I was paranoid about getting them mixed up. That's because bad things can happen if a bleeder set at 4 lbs. is inadvertently inserted into the right rear that should be set at 8 lbs., and then the right rear tire – now involuntarily bled down to 4 lbs. - has a high-speed confrontation with a heavy cushion.

Normally I inserted the right rear bleeder and attached its wheel-cover while at our pit stall just prior to being pushed to the staging area, watched the tire with a nervous eye, and just hoped it didn't bleed. This was due to issues we sometimes faced when installing the wheel cover on the right rear wheel.

Wheel-covers are used to prevent mud from accumulating inside the rim. Mud inside the rim can throw the wheel out of balance and cause the car to chatter something awful, along with the driver's teeth.

Normally they weren't needed on the left rear wheel, since the car blocks the mud as it slides through the corner. Except for the car-side of the wheel. Not much could be done about mud collecting there other than a hefty dousing of Mudd-Off.

Problems occasionally occurred if we were using a home-made wheel-cover, the hole pattern for the dzus buttons might line up only one way with the holes in the bead-lock, and a particular sized dzus button might need to be inserted into a particular hole. In short, you don't want to be dinking around with a wheel-cover in the staging area while they are pushing cars off, because it's not cool to be the one holding up the show, and they won't wait on you forever. However I would pop the right rear cover off and bleeder out in the staging area if there was a red flag in the race preceding ours, or there was some other delay.

Standing there in the staging area made for an interesting part of the night, and it was a place where I felt the gravity of the situation. There drivers sat in their cars "helmets on, buckled up" as they say, with game faces on preparing themselves to do battle.

Not that Jerry didn't have ways to break the tension sitting there, such as turning his head towards me with a bemused look in his eyes and saying something like, "I farted," which never failed to produce a guffaw out of me. Often I was the last person to see Jerry as he was pushed off for a race, and a little "off you go" thought would run through my mind.

As a pit crew we tried to station ourselves at different areas of the infield throughout the night in order to see how Jerry's car handled on different areas of the track. At that time Knoxville track officials allowed pit crew members to stand and watch the races on the outside of the chain link fence in the infield, right next to the Armco fence that ran along the inside of the track.

This was an awesome place to stand and something that never ceased to amaze me. I've never been able to definitively pinpoint exactly why I love sprint car racing so much, but one aspect of it had to do with the exhilaration felt standing next to the inside guardrail of turn three, watching the cars dive into the corner.

A mere few feet from the racing surface, those cars would scream by you at a dizzying speed - and I mean that literally. When a car races by that close at speeds well over 100 M.P.H. it makes you feel disoriented and somewhat dizzy.

It took some getting used to, and you definitely needed to keep your wits about you. One thing you don't ever want to do is turn your back on a sprint car, because they can be on top of you in an instant. Even in the pits I kept my head on a swivel and continuously looked over my shoulders.

For a while Knoxville put a stop to the practice of allowing us outside the chained link fence for safety reasons, or probably more accurately insurance reasons. When that happened I almost quit and took up fishing - I missed it that much. It was probably a good move on their part though, because in the past I had watched some flying debris from crashed sprint cars sail high over my head, standing that close to the track.

Standing in these areas also gave you a chance to observe other crews watching their cars on the track. I was always curious as to just what exactly future Hall of Fame car owner and mechanic Guy Forbrook looked at and thought of as he intensely studied the track or his car while it raced, but I never had the guts to ask.

When I stared at the track I might be trying to see if there was any moisture left, but I could just as likely be pondering if I should get the spicy or plain chicken bites at the concession stand. It was cool to see Forbrook drive by on his 4-wheeler and give him a respectful nod, and have him return one in kind, even though he didn't know me from Adam.

We completed these typical activities throughout the night unless, of course, we had problems. I wish I had kept a journal of all the issues we had because I think we experienced all of them. We could have published a "Complete Guide to Sprint Car Problems" book, or something to that effect.

Over the years we experienced blown engines, spindle breaks, fuel line problems, drive shaft breaks, lower shaft breaks, rear end gear breaks, stripped cam spuds, oil blowing out the breathers, fuel pick-up line collapses, fuel pump failures, rear axle stripped splines, overheating problems, engine timing problems, wrecks, and a host of other things I simply can't remember.

I don't believe these were caused by a lack of maintenance, as Jerry was naturally meticulous. More likely they were caused by using parts beyond their prime, which is not an uncommon affliction for the grassroots team.

After a problem occurred the diagnostics would normally commence after Jerry pulled into our pit stall, threw his driving gloves, neck collar, steering wheel, and/or helmet to the ground, and climbed out of the cockpit. This was followed by Jerry barking orders at and physically moving those of us in his way out of his way as he looked at a potential problem on the car or searched for a tool. My part of the process usually consisted of me staring blankly at a potential problem on the car, fetching tools, holding a part, or pointing a flashlight.

It was not a fun time to be around him. I don't hold it against him at all though because he was the one who had the money and sweat poured into his car, and whose butt was on the line in that car. After working many hours on the car throughout the week, mostly by himself, it pissed him off when something went wrong. Unfortunately, some of us were there to take the wrath.

On one occasion early in his sprint car career we were at Knoxville having problems trying to set the timing. Art Moose, from Moose Magnetos, was summoned to our pit stall by Jerry to help. As Jerry manned the timing light I held the magneto lock nut wrench on the nut ready to tighten it once the timing was set correctly.

Art tells me over the rumbling engine to advance the timing, which meant he wanted me to rotate the magneto in the direction that would advance the timing (in which direction, I had no idea). This can be tricky because if you rotate it too far the engine will die. Then we'd need to set the magneto back to a position where it was close, place the car in gear and push it backwards to get the fuel back out of the cylinders, flag down a push truck to start the car again, and repeat the timing process.

Exasperated that this was taking longer than it should, and not liking that he was doing this at the track, Jerry barked, "He doesn't know how to do that!" in a condescending tone.

Feeling offended I turned away and handed the wrench to Earl, who was standing behind me. I said, "Here you go, I've had enough," and I walked away for a while. Earl gave me a raised eyebrow look and grabbed the tool and took over.

I went to the front of the trailer where John was doing his "car owner duties" watching the races perched atop a ladder that led to the roof, and I whined. John's response to me was basically, "Whatever, get over it."

The next week at the shop Earl said something to Jerry about him being hard to work with because his crew guys were handing their tools away to bystanders at the track. Evidently Jerry hadn't paid much attention to the timing setting fiasco, because he acted like he didn't know what Earl was talking about.

Jerry had every right to be ticked off though, because I really didn't know how to advance the timing. Little things like that bothered me during Jerry's early sprint car racing years, bruising my young ego more than anything, but as I matured I didn't think anything of them.

Actually I began to enjoy episodes like these because they were excellent opportunities to observe Jerry in his natural old-school state.

More stressful moments occurred when Jerry was involved in an accident and the car was damaged, but not too damaged to call it a night.

It is a sinking feeling experienced in the pit of your stomach when you're standing next to the fence in the infield watching your car go by, lap after lap, and you know what position it is in, and then the yellow comes out. That sinking feeling worsens after you watch the cars go by that were not involved, realize your car is not in the position it was in prior to said yellow flag, and therefore must be involved.

After that happened and you made the mad dash to the car parked in your pit stall or work area, the well-known term, "thrashing," came into play.

If there was such a thing as a racing slang dictionary I believe the definition of thrashing, at least in this context, would be something along the lines of, "The half-assed fixing of a broken race car with the unrealistic expectation of returning said race car to a racing event in a competitive state."

If we had time to fix the car before the next race of the night it wasn't so bad. If it was during a red flag stop, you really didn't have much time to work.

One year during the Masters Classic, the race for drivers 50 years old and older held at Knoxville during Hall of Fame induction weekend, Jerry became involved in an accident during the feature which caused some damage to his car. They threw the red flag and I knew that since this was a high paying race, at least for our standards, he would want to get back out and race if there was any chance to fix the car.

After they pulled him into the work area, and with Jerry still strapped in, we found two main problems with the car. One was that a top wing side panel support had snapped in half. The other was that the front torsion tube had a big dent in it, preventing the torsion bar from twisting. This means there was no suspension travel in the front of the car. If you stood on the front end, it was just solid.

Fortunately when things like this happen you receive a lot of help from other crews whose cars aren't in the race or weren't involved in the accident. For the broken wing side panel support a decision was made to position the two broken ends together, place a wrench parallel to them across the break, and duct tape the crap out of it (see previous definition of "thrashing").

A track official was there and even he was okay with the temporary fix, which was somewhat disconcerting, although a broken side panel support really isn't that big of a deal. There wasn't anything that could be done with the torsion tube in the short amount of time we had. The track was cleared, the yellow flag replaced the red, and they pushed Jerry back out onto the track.

Nelson and I ran to the trailer and fetched the spare top wing to replace the damaged one in case there was another red flag. As we carried the wing back to the work area we heard the race restart and then abruptly stop, due to another red flag.

Our hopes of replacing the wing were immediately dashed when we learned that the red was for Jerry, as he had hit the fence in turn two and dumped his car, flipping it end over end.

We didn't find out if the "wrench fix" would have held, since Jerry's flip happened on the first lap of the restart. The bent torsion tube was likely the culprit in this case since there was no travel in the front suspension, therefore no weight transfer, and probably caused the car to push right into the fence.

Jerry later said he forgot all about the damage to the torsion tube when the green flag flew on the restart and he just stood on the throttle. It was all just as well though because upon further inspection of the spare wing we discovered that the mounting structure beneath the wing was installed backwards. That would have caused problems if we had tried to mount it atop Jerry's car during a red flag.

Billy Englehart ended up winning The Masters that night.

When people asked me what I did for Jerry in the pits, I usually responded, "Whatever he wants me to do." I mentioned this to him once and he just said, "That's good, because that's what I need." That's probably why he never ran me off during all those years.

It did get to the point where he would pull in and either subtlety nod towards or slightly flick a finger or thumb at an area of the car, and I would immediately know what he wanted done - whether it be removing the hood, jacking up the car, changing a shock or tire, or whatever. Whenever that happens you realize you've been around someone a long time and communication is on point.

And don't read too much into the issues we had completing any of the above duties. They could go off without a hitch 99 times out of 100. But that one time it didn't was the one you remembered, and it was usually the funny one.

After the races were over we usually hung out for a while and talked with other crews, drivers, and fans as they mingled in the pits. It was fun to watch little kids who ran from trailer to trailer seeking drivers' autographs. I always enjoyed the surprised and confused look on their faces when after they asked, "Who drives this car?" John would point to Jerry and say, "That bald-headed old fart over there." They would hesitate a moment until someone confirmed John's statement.

Inevitably, Jerry would hold out his Sharpie and say, "Where do you want me to sign?" But before they could answer he would take the pen with the lid still on and pretend to sign their little foreheads. This would produce astonished and worried looks on their faces, until they realized the ruse. Laughing, Jerry would tussle their hair and then give them a proper signature on their shirt, paper, or whatever item they held in their hands.

Many would want to sit in the car, which was always a treat for the youngsters. The look in their eyes when they realized they were sitting in a car they had just watched on the track was simply priceless. It was one of awe. I'm glad the sport hasn't grown too much and this type of thing can still occur. I'm sure I've unknowingly watched some future sprint car drivers sit in Jerry's car.

Once the crowd began to disperse we would pack up the trailer and load the car, finishing anywhere from a five to eight hour or longer night. Funny how in the earlier days, when Jerry did well, we would hang around for a while. But later, when he was struggling, we tended to pack up and leave immediately after the races. Maybe it was because we were all just getting older.

As soon as everything was loaded and the trailer buttoned up, I would bid farewell and make my way to the pit gate. Walking outside the track in the glow of the Musco lighting always made me a bit melancholy, feeling a little sad that the races were over for the night, but already looking forward to the next weekend. The walk to my car and drive home gave me a chance to think over and replay the night's events in my head.

After I got home, cleaned up, peeked in on my sleeping kids, and crawled into bed, I could still hear the roar of the engines ringing in my ears.

Why on earth would anyone do this? Racing really does get into your blood. I think it all comes down to camaraderie: camaraderie with the drivers, people in your pit crew and others', officials, 4-wheeler drivers, push truck drivers, fans - everybody. Because everybody there is doing something they love to do.

**Jerry back in the day riding his handcrafted 3-wheeler.
(J.R. Photo's)**

**Jerry riding his #12 handcrafted 3-wheeler.
(Bryan Raffa photo)**

Jerry with his 3-wheeler in recent years at the "Battle at the Barn" Coke syrup races in the Richard O. Jacobson Exhibition Center on the Iowa State Fairgrounds. (Randy Smith photo)

Top view of Jerry's handcrafted 3-wheeler.
(Randy Smith photo)

The first car Jerry drove at Knoxville in 1990. This is the car 4-wheeler driver Dave Cornwell said was the heaviest he ever pushed. Pretty car, though. (Jan Crabb collection)

Jerry in his own car at Knoxville in 1991. This car was destroyed later that year at the start of a heat race. (J.R. Photo's)

Jerry at Knoxville. This may have been 1993 during the
inaugural Masters Classic, then known as the Hall of Fame
Classic. (National Sprint Car Hall of Fame & Museum
collection)

Inaugural Masters Classic podium in 1993. L-R: Tom Schmeh,
Archie Ergenbright, Rick Ferkel, and Jerry Crabb.
(National Sprint Car Hall of Fame & Museum collection)

Inaugural Masters Classic podium in 1993. L-R: Archie Ergenbright, 3rd, Rick Ferkel, 1st, and Jerry Crabb, 2nd. (National Sprint Car Hall of Fame & Museum collection)

Mike Thomas and Jerry at the inaugural Masters Classic in 1993. (National Sprint Car Hall of Fame & Museum collection)

Jerry posing with the car near his shop on SW 9th, likely 1993.
(Jan Crabb collection)

Jerry's crash at the 1996 Masters Classic, which occurred on the
restart after a previous incident left the car with a dented front
torsion tube. There's a duct-taped wrench in there somewhere.
(National Sprint Car Hall of Fame & Museum collection)

Jerry at Knoxville in later years.
(National Sprint Car Hall of Fame & Museum collection)

Jerry at Knoxville in later years.
(National Sprint Car Hall of Fame & Museum collection)

Jerry and Jan in victory lane at the Iowa State Fairgrounds in 1997, his second win at the track. (Dean Malone photo)

Podium at the 1998 Masters Classic. L-R: Billy Engelhart, 3rd, Jerry Crabb, 1st, Kathy Visser, John Bankston, 2nd. (National Sprint Car Hall of Fame & Museum collection)

Jerry and flagman Norm Wadle following the 1998 Masters Classic. (National Sprint Car Hall of Fame & Museum collection)

My favorite photo because Jerry is on the left side of the car working, and Tracie, Jan, and I are on the right side screwing around. (author's collection)

Jan takes a turn at the wheel. Jerry on the left, Tracie at right.
(Jan Crabb collection)

The crew in later years: Tracie, Todd, Shane, and Jan.
(Jan Crabb collection)

The John Allen sprinter. (author's photo)

My first car starting experience, Earl Terry on the left.
(author's collection)

The Crabb homestead at "Crabby Acres" in southern Iowa.
Jerry did a majority of the construction, at age 65.
(author's photo)

The shed at "Crabby Acres." That's the old motor home parked
alongside. (author's photo)

The sign that once hung at Jerry's TV shop on SW 9th, and now hangs on the door to his man cave. (author's photo)

Not sure which spectacular crash this award refers to, he had more than one at the fairgrounds. (author's photo)

Jerry's number plate for winning the "Over 30 Cycle" points championship during the 1986-1987 Winter Dome season. (author's photo)

The 1998 Masters Classic trophy. (author's photo)

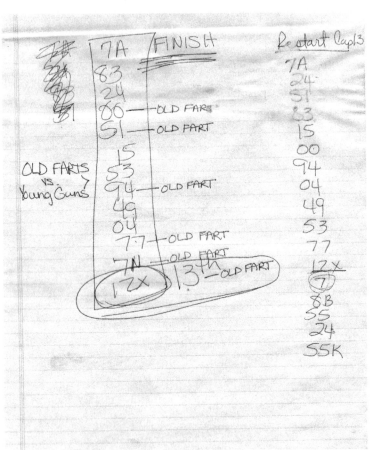

The 2006 Young Guns vs. Masters feature finish from Jan's records. Interesting how the "Masters" participants are identified. (author's photo)

I'm told this is the chassis that won the 1998 Masters Classic.
I'm also told a restoration project is in the works.
(author's photo)

Jerry's second trailer. We spent a lot of time in there.
(author's photo)

"Captain," Jerry's mule. It seems fitting that he would own a stubborn ole' mule. I understand Jerry only rode him one time, and was a bit nervous during the ride. I surmise this is because it is an animal with its own mind, rather than a machine Jerry could control. (author's photo)

Jerry celebrating a birthday, stationed in Korea in the 1960's. (Jan Crabb collection)

Jan and Jerry, December 2017. (Jan Crabb collection)

Twedt's first car wore Trostle's famous #20. This photo was taken during one of my trips to Huxley to help polish the car. (author's photo)

Twedt's car at a car show inside a mall in Oskaloosa, Danny Young's car in the background. This is the photo I submitted to *Open Wheel Magazine*, which appeared in the "In-Out Box" section of the October 1988 issue. (author's photo)

Mike always included a shadowy silhouette portrait of Jesse
James on both sides of the hood. That's Mike in the
background above the hood. (author's photo)

I was thrilled when Mike had my name painted on the hood of
his car. Note Ted Hulgan's name is there too, among others.
(author's photo)

Sometimes Bad Things Happen

"A sprint car is racing's answer to a lit stick of dynamite," Dr. Dick Berggren once said while describing a sprint car during one of those old television broadcasts. That's one of the greatest descriptions I've ever heard. I've also heard them described as engine stands on wheels. That's pretty good too. However you describe them one thing is for certain - they have to be one of the most wicked racing vehicles on earth.

Lightweight and extremely over-horsepowered, a 410 cubic inch sprint car has around the same horsepower-to-weight ratio as that of a Formula 1 car. Consisting of a tubular chromoly frame, fuel injected open header engine sitting in front of the driver, with the driveline running from the engine through a torque tube between the driver's legs to reach the solid rear axle - they are hell on wheels.

There is no self-starting system. For the most part there is nothing on a sprint car that doesn't make it go faster, other than safety equipment. Four open wheels with a small wing on the front and a large one on top, which creates down force to hold them to the ground, these cars can reach top speed in the blink of an eye. These things are all race car, and allow their drivers to race with a frantic sense of urgency.

When you place several of these twitchy race cars on the track at once it can sometimes be a recipe for disaster. Every driver who straps into one of these machines knows that at some point they will inevitably become involved in an accident.

Due to the open wheels, lightweight design, and enormous horsepower, many times these cars perform spectacular flips. I don't agree with the theory that people go to sprint car races to see crashes. People who go to sprint car races are generally a pretty sophisticated bunch, at least as far as sprint car racing is concerned. They realize the danger involved and have a good idea of how much it costs to fix a bent-up race car. Plus they don't like the delay in the show that occurs while the track is being cleared.

After all, they're sprint car fans – with the emphasis on the word "sprint." They like their entertainment now, with intensity, and over and done with so they can get home at a decent hour. There are a few idiots in every crowd, but for the most part sprint car people do not enjoy seeing crashes.

That being said, whenever accidents happen everyone cranes their necks to see them and are disappointed if they miss them. It's simple human nature and much like rubbernecking at a highway accident. Without a doubt, a sprint car crash is visually stimulating.

The sound of a sprint car crash is one that has no comparison and is difficult to describe. It is a sickening, evil, explosive impact sound which occurs when fiberglass, carbon fiber, aluminum, and steel - traveling at a high rate of speed in close formation - meets another such formation or Armco fence.

Then those who witness the incident talk about, rehash, and dissect the wreck, trying to determine if someone was at fault or if it was "just racing." They recall accidents that happened years ago.

I must admit, I do this too.

I'll never forget the crash involving Dave Blaney, John Sernett, Danny Thoman, and Marlon Jones during the 1988 Knoxville Nationals. Right after taking the green flag in a heat race those four became entangled racing into turn one and hit the fence like a freight train. The four mashed into a cloud of dirt, smoke, sprint car parts, fence parts, and God only knows what else. In addition to seeing it with my own eyes I've watched the videotape 100 times, and I never could tell exactly what happened in that vicious ball of yuck. Marlon Jones' car bashed its way through the old wooden fence and ended up just north of the spectator restroom on the east end of the grandstand. Flagman Doug Clark climbed down from his flag stand and ran to Jones' car, I suppose because he was the closest official on the grandstand side of the fence. I'm not sure how nobody was injured in that one.

It took track officials a long time to repair the damage enough to resume racing that night, and that was the first time I saw track workers use a chainsaw to cut a new board for the fence. The delay did help Dave Blaney though, as his crew guys and about a hundred others defied my definition of thrashing and were able to make repairs to his car. He ended up winning the feature that night.

I also won't forget the time Jimmy Evans launched his car out of the park at Knoxville, over the fence between the billboards and scoreboard in turn three as I watched from the inside guardrail near there. I don't know how it started, but once in the air his bright yellow car took off like an airplane. After they opened the pit gate for the rescue crew I wandered out to take a look. His car appeared very small and out of place sitting next to the drive leading to the pits outside turns three and four.

I will always remember the time Larry Weeks sent his car into the timber off the backstretch in Webster City, Iowa. Jerry was correct when he described that after the timber swallowed up Larry's car, it appeared as if the timber spit back pieces of his car one at a time. Jerry may have been involved in that incident somehow, as I recall swapping out a damaged shock for a good one during the ensuing red flag stop.

Of course, Jerry could not escape this affliction associated with the sport.

The first car he owned was said to be a Tognotti, although no one knew for sure, not even the guy who sold it to him. The frame was heavy, painted dark blue, and it appeared that the down tubes (bars on each side of the frame that run from the top front of the roll cage to the front of the frame) were not original equipment and welded on later in the car's life. The frame simply appeared to be, well, brittle. But he assembled it and raced it, and as far as he could tell it worked just fine.

That is until one night at Knoxville during a heat race when

Jerry started on the pole.

The green flag flew at the start of the race and Jerry and the outside front row starter dove into turn one side by side. Jerry held his line, but the guy on the outside moved down the track and got into Jerry's right front wheel. This caused the whole front end assembly to collapse on the car.

All hell broke loose at that point. The front of the frame dug into the dirt and tripped the car, sending Jerry through a series of twisting and turning flips. At one point, while upside down and sideways in midair in the middle of the track, a car that started behind him sheared off the front of his car in front of the radiator. Another following car somersaulted over him and somehow landed on its wheels. A trail of parts and debris scattered the track as Jerry's car came to a rest on its side.

Smooth and I happened to be standing at the inside guardrail in turns one and two and witnessed the incident firsthand. I cowered behind the guardrail as the accident progressed, kneeling down almost as if I could protect myself from it happening.

We simultaneously said, "Oh (insert well-known curse word here)!" and then stayed there for a moment in silence as the rescue crew quickly made their way to the scene.

One thing about Knoxville - I believe they have one of the best rescue crews in any form of racing, anywhere in the world. They like to have fun, but they take their jobs very, very seriously. I'll never forget the time Steve Breazeale crashed exiting turn two and his car burst into flames, as I watched from the backstretch perched on the front bumper of Jerry's motor home. The rescue crew guys in that corner were Johnny-on-the-spot administering flame retardant until the fire truck arrived. Once on the scene a rescue crewmember literally walked into a wall of flames without any hesitation to help Steve out of the car. It was an amazing sight to see.

Back to Jerry's accident, we stood and waited until we could see him unbuckling his safety belts. At that point we jumped over the inside guardrail and - doing what everyone helping with a car in those days did when the track allowed pit crews onto the track during red flag stops - ran to the scene and stood there.

Strange. I've noticed this behavior before. I have the

videotape *Up and Over* hosted by Doug Wolfgang, which shows sprint car accidents from the Midwest. In almost every instance the crew members, if allowed on the track, ran to the scene of the accident and just stood there for a few moments. It must have something to do with the shock factor.

Anyway, Jerry was not injured and simply crawled out and took an assessment of his destroyed race car, which now only consisted of the engine, roll cage, rear axle, and fuel tank.

He later said that while he was flipping and the welds of the down tubes broke and flailed about, that he thought those pieces of metal were trying to stab him on purpose. They wouldn't get a second chance though, as this car was junk. To this day people bring up that first wreck of his.

Then there was the time Jerry decided to enter the IMCA Nationals at Boone Speedway in Boone, Iowa, I think at the urging of Booby Thompson. I wasn't exactly thrilled with the prospect because the practice night for sprint cars was on a weeknight, and I wasn't pleased with the idea of spending a late night just to make some practice laps and then have to wake up early the next morning to go to work. But, Boone Speedway is a racy little high-banked quarter-mile joint, and in reality any time spent at the races was usually time well spent.

So Smoothie and I helped Jerry load up the trailer and we headed north on I-35, on the way to Boone. We arrived at the pit gate and paid for our pit passes, which seemed unfair since we were only going to make some practice laps. However, since this was an event with what seemed like a zillion different classes competing all week long - our practice would happen in between a couple of events - we still had to pay.

Instead of whining we nodded in acknowledgement to the "No Crybabies Allowed" sign posted at the pit gate, drove in, and parked next to Booby's trailer. I thought we were in the wrong place, as I could not see any other sprint cars in the vicinity. I soon found out the reason why: Booby and Jerry were the only two sprint car drivers to show up for practice. I should have seen that as a bad omen.

When our time came to practice Booby and Jerry were pushed out onto the track. Jerry had never raced a sprint car on a high-banked bullring like this one, so he followed Booby at about a quarter lap back as they idled around the track on their warm-up laps.

Booby took the green flag around halfway down the back straight as Jerry was in the middle of turns one and two. Boob hammered the throttle and streaked through turns three and four. Jerry's car screamed down the back chute and entered turn three.

But instead of streaking through three and four as Booby's car had, Jerry's car drifted, and drifted, and drifted higher on the track, until suddenly it hopped over the top of the banking in turns three and four.

Since there were no guardrails surrounding the corners at Boone Speedway at the time, this was not an uncommon sight. In fact, there were many a time that I witnessed cars disappearing over the embankment, only to see them pop back onto the track and merge in with the racing traffic on the following straightaway. The only harm done was the loss of a few positions. In Jerry's case, after disappearing over the embankment, my eyes tried to follow ahead and imagine where he was and where he might pop back onto the track.

That is until my eyes stopped at a track light pole that appeared to be directly in the line Jerry's car had taken off the track.

A split second later that light pole, which was a telephone pole, shuddered violently. A couple of seconds later, after the pole stopped shuddering and the packed grandstands finished their collective gasp, a single large light bulb dropped straight down and put a period to the end of Jerry's practice run.

Stunned, Smooth and I looked at each other, shrugged our shoulders, and headed to the trailer to await Jerry's return. Luckily, Jerry was uninjured. Unfortunately what the tow truck towed back looked more like a banana than a sprint car, as Jerry's car was broadside when it made contact with the light pole and now resembled that fruit. We did not make a return trip to the IMCA Nationals that year.

Likely because I tried to block it from memory, I only vaguely recall a faux pas that occurred one year at a race in Burlington, Iowa. Jerry was leading the feature until a late-race yellow, which was when Nelson and I noticed the air in his right rear tire had decided to quit early for the night.

We dragged the jack, wheel wrench, and spare right rear to

the work area. But Jerry opted to try and limp through the rest of the race on the nearly flat tire, rather than change it and restart at the tail of the field.

Apparently the flagman forgot his black flag that evening and went ahead and threw the green for the restart. The melee that ensued due to Jerry trying to race on a flat tire resulted in the sole instance where we had to hustle to load the car, button up the trailer, and get the hell out of Dodge before the locals had a chance to gather pitchforks and light torches. On the way back we kept an eye on the sideview mirrors of the motor home until we were well outside city limits.

A few years ago the SCRA, one of the wingless sprint car organizations, scheduled a race at Knoxville. There have not been very many non-winged sprint car races at Knoxville in recent years, but when they do hold an event there are usually a few of the Knoxville regulars who remove the wings from their cars and try to race with the wingless guys.

The regulars have experienced mixed results, sometimes disastrous. The previous year one of the locals who competed flipped his car violently in turn one. When a wingless car crashes, without the big wing to cushion the initial blow, they sometimes flip for days. Rumor had it that when the local driver drove into the corner he forgot he didn't have a wing on top. Jerry didn't understand how that could happen.

This non-winged idea intrigued Jerry. I think he thought that since he had a great deal of experience racing 3-wheelers and 4-wheelers, which of course do not have wings, racing a sprint car without a wing would be similar. A wing holds the car down, increases traction, improves handling, and multiplies the importance of a strong engine many times over. Without a wing the driver becomes more important and strong engines are somewhat neutralized, since there is a greater tendency to spin the tires.

So, Jerry showed up for this race. I, for one, was excited. I was going to be able to watch drivers I had read about but didn't have the opportunity to see very often. Non-winged races tend to be close and competitive. And I loved watching the drivers back their cars in entering the corners, sometimes with the left front tire barely touching the ground. I was psyched.

We pulled into the pits and parked next to Jay Drake, a very well-known and exceptional non-wing sprint car driver. After unloading the car and equipment we strolled over and took a look at his car. That was when I started having a few doubts, and my worrying began in earnest.

Jay's car was offset to the left a bunch more than ours. His left front torsion arm had a large indention, which would allow him to turn farther to the right if the car became too sideways. Our torsion arm was straight. His right rear tire was spaced out way farther than ours was even capable of doing. His left rear tire was sucked in close to the car due to a special radius rod and torsion arm. The stagger was less than anything we could even come close to. In short, he had a car designed for non-wing racing, and we just had a winged car minus the wings.

"Let's move the left rear in as close as we can, the right out as far as we can, and use as little stagger as possible," was Jerry's plan for his own car.

We did the best we could with what we had and prepared the car for hot laps. Jerry's hot lap session was called to the push off area and he was pushed out onto the track. It was pretty cool to see him out there, sans wings.

He idled around the track a few laps and took the green flag midway through the back straight. Although he was not up to top speed, he looked good racing through turns three and four and appeared to get a good bite coming out of four. Due to other trailers in the way we lost sight of him going down the front straight, so we focused our attention on the back straight and waited for him to exit turn two.

But then the red flag came out. Jan and I looked at each other. Then the announcer announced that Jerry had flipped his car entering turn one. Jan ran to turn one and I started looking for jack stands to set the car on. The tow truck towed Jerry's car back to our pit stall and placed it on the jack stands. Other than some broken bars the car really didn't appear to be hurt all that bad, but there was no way we would be racing the rest of the night.

After inspecting the car, Jerry remarked, "At least we didn't hurt the wings."

I asked Jerry whether he forgot he didn't have a wing on the car when he entered turn one. I didn't receive a straight answer. Jay Drake went on to win the feature that night, and a person could view nearly the entire spectrum of sprint car racing looking back and forth between our side by side pit stalls.

It was at the Iowa State Fair Speedway in Des Moines where Jerry displayed one of his most spectacular accidents. I didn't particularly enjoy going to the fairgrounds to race very much, mostly because Knoxville spoils you, but also partly because it was a bit disconcerting that their "ambulance" could not leave fairgrounds property.

I say "ambulance" because the vehicle looked suspiciously like a normal passenger van that someone painted to look "ambulance-y." So if a driver needed to go to the hospital they would load the poor guy in the "ambulance" and rush him to the main gate of the fairgrounds. They would wait there until the real ambulance showed up, and then hand off the driver to the real one.

I suppose I would have appreciated racing at the fairgrounds more if I had known they were going to rip out over 100 years of auto racing history right along with the track in 2016. This was the track that caused Mario Andretti's twin brother Aldo to call it a career after suffering serious injuries there during a vicious sprint car accident in 1969. Now it joins a growing list of dirt tracks that no longer exist.

One year a sprint car race was held on a weeknight during the Iowa State Fair and Jerry entered to race. At the drop of the green flag of his heat race he immediately jumped out to a several car length lead. Stretching his lead down the backstretch, for some reason his car drifted up the track and made contact with the wall right before entering turn three.

That area was only protected by an Armco fence. On the other side of the fence it dropped down a few feet to a road that ran alongside the parking lot, which was usually packed with fair-goers' cars.

After making contact with the wall, Jerry's car launched. In midair, with the top of the wing facing the infield, the car made sort of a lazy 270-degree cartwheel. You could clearly see the large red 12x painted on the top of the wing before it disappeared on the other side of the fence.

I'm not sure what happened on the other side of the fence, but you could vaguely see parts and pieces and debris just sort of popping up into the air. The car came to rest in a pile of pea gravel, and Jerry noted afterwards that he was completely covered with gravel and dust after his car came to rest.

I imagine a couple of fair-goers who parked in the area were surprised upon arriving at their vehicles to depart that night, as some sprint car shrapnel went through the window of one car and a wheel wiped out the side of a sport utility vehicle. I do not know if Jerry's wreck had anything to do with it, but that was the last time they raced winged sprint cars during the Iowa State Fair.

I was not in attendance that night, but did have the opportunity to view this accident every night for a week for several years. This is because they showed the replay of his crash nightly during the intro of the Iowa Public Television broadcast of Iowa State Fair highlights. For a while it appeared in the "Thrills and Spills" section of the video montage. Then I believe it was under the heading of "Death Defying Stunts," or something to that effect.

I know for a fact that every year at least one person brought it up to Jerry that they had watched his accident on TV during the Fair highlight shows. He didn't seem to enjoy reminiscing about it.

The majority of times after an accident everyone holds their breath for a few moments until the driver unbuckles, crawls out of his bent-up race car, and dusts himself off. He may be wobbly, shaken, or just plain ticked off, but for the most part he is okay. The next day he may be stiff and sore, sport bruises where his shoulder belts dug into his flesh, and might have red eyes caused by blood vessels bursting due to centrifugal forces, but not suffering any long-term effects. Unfortunately this is not always the case.

For a few years one of our sponsors, Mark Detrick, decided he wanted to give sprint car racing a try. He raced motocross some in his younger days, but since becoming a sprint car fan and sponsor, he had the desire to get behind the wheel of one of these machines.

So Mark and Jerry built a second car for Mark to drive, assembled from a spare frame and several spare parts accumulated over the years. And let me tell you, Mark had a blast. He wasn't in contention to win a race, but did show improvement, and he had fun. He simply wanted to experience the thrill of driving a sprint car.

One Saturday night at Knoxville Mark was racing in the B main while I busied myself at our trailer in the pits. I hadn't paid a whole lot of attention to the race, but as I walked up the ramp of the trailer I happened to glance at the track in turns three and four, just in time to see Mark tag the wall and take a couple of end over end flips. It wasn't the worst crash I had ever seen, but definitely a hard hitting one, with the ends of the car pounding and digging into the track on each revolution.

Mark was stiff and sore and wobbly when he returned to his pit stall, which was right next to ours. The bruises on his shoulders from the safety belts were seeping blood, and he was having trouble seeing.

He went to the doctor the following week and it was discovered that he had a wrinkled retina in one of his eyes. Because of this, basically there is just a part of his vision that is not there anymore, and it's probably permanent. That is an awfully high price to pay for going out to have fun, but I never heard Mark complain about it one bit and I really don't think he regrets it at all.

Sometimes the absolute worst happens. Nobody likes to talk about it, but it is in the back of your mind. It's easy to put in the back of your mind, especially when you're at the races and everyone is having a good time and enjoying themselves. I think that is why it is such a shock when tragedy strikes.

I was at Jerry's shop loading barrels to make a fuel run early on a Saturday morning when I heard about Doug Wolfgang's accident at Lakeside Speedway in Kansas City. The World of Outlaws held a practice at the track, which was paved at the time, because they had only raced on that type of surface a few instances in their history.

During a practice run Wolfgang clipped a tractor tire that was placed on the inside of the track and the front end of his car collapsed, sending him hard into the outside retaining wall.

A fire ensued and was fed by a fuel leak in his damaged car, and he was unconscious.

The track rescue personnel were unable to extract him from the car or stop the fire. Some estimates say that he sat in the burning race car anywhere from five to ten minutes, and it took the efforts of a couple of his fellow drivers in their fire suits to pull him out. He was severely burned, in addition to having a concussion and other broken bones. He also breathed in a lot of toxic fumes as he sat in the burning car.

After a long recovery he did make a return to racing and experienced some success, although not to the extent he was accustomed to prior to his accident. Regardless, he'll always be my all-time favorite driver.

It was a consolation feature during the Knoxville Nationals one year when Curtis Boyer destroyed his car right before my eyes as I watched the races from the back of John's pickup truck in turn three. The body language of the rescue crew indicated the seriousness of his injuries, and they covered the car with a white sheet before hauling it to the cattle barn after extricating the unconscious driver. Rumors ran rampant about his condition the rest of the night.

Thankfully, Mr. Boyer survived. An article by Doug Auld in *Sprint Car & Midget Magazine* several months later stated that Curtis was revived several times that night and he suffered through a long recovery. Curtis said he had a near death experience, lived to spread the word of God, was almost fully recovered, and planned to return to racing the following season.

I was horrified to see him nearly a year after his crash involved in an identical accident at almost the exact same spot on the track. However that time he hopped right out and dusted himself off.

I was on my way to work on a Thursday morning when I heard on the radio that Danny Young had been killed in a sprint car accident at Knoxville during the previous night's World of Outlaws race.

Danny was a big kid from the rough and tumble east side of Des Moines and worked for the family tree service business. Rumor had it that in a disagreement he once went after someone with a chainsaw – I don't know if that was true but it wouldn't have surprised me. A former champion go-cart racer, he was an up-and-coming star in the sprint car ranks – both 360 and 410 classes. During the years he raced at the State Fair Speedway he won all but a few races he entered.

He made the mainstream news on a Friday night one year when a helicopter was rented to fly him back and forth between a 360 race at the fairgrounds and a World of Outlaws show in Knoxville. Somehow they pulled that off - he won two features at the fairgrounds, and won his heat race and finished 15th in the feature with the Outlaws in Knoxville.

Danny's team was family owned, and wherever Danny went his father Butch was not far behind. You always knew where Butch was, for his high-pitched voice seemed to carry across the pits, even above running engines. You could tell when Butch and Danny argued, which was a nightly occurrence, because the decibel level of Butch's voice somehow increased. But they loved racing and the way they did it, and rather than receive the first-place check for winning a race I believe they would have paid that amount just to enter a race.

I cannot say I knew Danny and his family, but Jerry did, simply from being at the same racetracks so many times. Their presence in our pit stall was a regular occurrence, especially at the fairgrounds.

At one track Jerry got to know Butch a little too well. The story goes that Danny was leading the yellow flag plagued feature, which caused several cars to run dry of methanol fuel, which caused even more yellow flags as cars continued to stop on the track, fuel tanks empty. Eventually Jerry became one of the afflicted and stopped on the track. Butch didn't appreciate the delay and went after Jerry. A crewmember got in between the two, but somehow Butch reached around the guy and popped Jerry in the nose. But, for the most part, Jerry and the Youngs got along just fine.

At Danny's funeral Jerry offered his condolences to Butch, who simply replied, "We sure had a lot of fun, didn't we." At Knoxville on the Saturday following Danny's death everyone in the infield wore black ribbons, lined the front stretch, and joined hands in a moment of silence. You still see 3Y stickers on race cars and passenger cars, referencing the car number and memory of Danny Young.

I was in church on a Sunday morning when I heard that Mark Wilson died during practice at Knoxville the previous night. Mark was hotlapping a car owned by Larry Weeks, who had retired from driving by that time. It seems a part failed on the car and sent Mark into the fence near the south pit gate.

The thing everyone knew about Mark was that he was Bob Trostle's grandson, which had to put a tremendous amount of pressure on the kid. And you could tell he came from some fine racing genes, as he won his fair share of races. I loved watching him at the fairgrounds, where he would literally back his car in entering turn one, without lifting his foot off the throttle. I did not know Mark or his grandfather personally, but he appeared to be a decent and modest young man.

There's something to be said about Bob also, as he continued to field a car at Knoxville. He simply could not turn his back away from the sport he has been such an instrumental part of for so many years. In many ways, Trostle is Knoxville, and Knoxville is Trostle, and it wouldn't be the same to not see him patrolling the pit area.

At Knoxville if you walk into the pits through the small gate just on the west end of the south grandstand, and look to the ground at the right of the entrance, you can see a small memorial to Mark. You also still see many "God Bless Mark Wilson" stickers on the windows of passenger cars and on the sides of sprint cars.

I remember learning when Brad Doty was paralyzed at Eldora, watching on ESPN as Rich Vogler took his final lap and win, and hearing the description of the horrific accident that took Keith Hutton's life at Oskaloosa. I remember hearing about Kevin Gobrecht in Nebraska. All of these and many more serve as serious reminders of what can happen when a driver gets behind the wheel of a sprint car.

Unfortunately Jerry could not avoid becoming involved in this type of incident.

One Saturday night at Knoxville Jerry started on the pole of the feature. At the drop of the green flag a car zoomed around Jerry on the top side in one and two. A couple laps later another car passed Jerry, and then another. Jerry stayed in fourth place for several circuits and seemed to be holding his own, until the 1K car of Minnesotan Billy Anderson, in fifth place, closed the gap.

I'm not sure what lap it was, but as the two cars raced toward turn one Billy tried to pass Jerry on the high side. He made contact with Jerry's right rear tire and began a series of some of the most violent end over end flips I have ever witnessed, right in front of the grandstand. It seemed never-ending, as he flipped over and over, his car disintegrating. It took the rescue crew several minutes to extract him from the car.

At the time I didn't know Jerry was involved. All that I could see from my position in turn four was Anderson's car flipping. So I was shocked when someone yelled that we needed a new right rear, and when they towed Jerry's car to the work area I saw that only the center section of the wheel remained on the axle. We bolted on another right rear and they pushed him off. He restarted at the tail of the field and finished the race.

After the race and back at our pit stall we began to hear rumors about Billy Anderson, and it was not good. On the way home I searched radio stations to try and find news, but of course there wasn't any at that late hour.

The next day I read in the paper that Billy Anderson was alive, but had to be resuscitated several times on the way to, and at, Knoxville Community Hospital. He was air-lifted to Mercy Hospital in Des Moines and resuscitated more times. It was reported that his third and fourth vertebrae were fractured and he was paralyzed from the neck down, but he was alive.

I feared the possibility that Jerry had caused the wreck, because from where I stood in turn four I could not see the initial contact with my own eyes. Later I heard that Knoxville Raceway officials reviewed a videotape of the accident and they determined it to be simply a racing incident. That didn't help Billy Anderson, or the fact that our race team was involved.

A week later I read an article by Jeff Olson, who covered auto racing for *The Des Moines Register* at the time. He wrote, "Blame serves no purpose here. It wasn't, as some have suggested, the car's fault. It wasn't Knoxville Raceway's fault, it wasn't Jerry Crabb's fault, it wasn't the neck brace's fault, it wasn't Billy Anderson's fault. It was, plain and simple, an accident. As callous as it sounds, it's still a part of sprint-car racing. This isn't bowling. It's a brutally dangerous sport."

Tragically, Billy Anderson succumbed to complications from his injuries a few years later.

I believe Mr. Olsen had it right. It is a dangerous sport and horrible things can happen. The article also mentioned about how in the old days, the days before roll cages and wings, some drivers who traveled the country carried a dress suit with them to wear to the funerals of fellow drivers that were sure to occur during the season. It was not uncommon to lose one or two drivers in a weekend.

Fortunately, in this day and age with the safety rules and equipment that exist, it doesn't happen as often as it did in the past. But when it does, it is uncommon enough that it truly shocks us.

"Think You Can Do This?"

"You want to start the car tonight?" Jerry asked me casually one night at Knoxville, as he sported an ornery grin.

"Uh, okay," I replied, trying to sound nonchalant and keep my heart, which instantaneously went from a rate of around 60 to 250 beats per minute, out of my throat.

I turned away quickly and tried to visualize the starting process in my mind, but wasn't thinking straight. Do I place the car in gear, turn on the fuel, and then flip the mag switch? Or is it gear, mag switch, and then fuel? How much oil pressure does the engine need to build before I flip the switch?

"You're going to run through this with me a couple of times, right?" I asked Jerry, failing in my attempt to sound confident.

"What?" he fired back. "You know how to do this. Put the car in gear, turn on the fuel, wait until you build up about 40 pounds of oil pressure, tap the throttle a couple times, flip the mag switch, and that's it."

I nodded and turned away again, my mind racing.

Great. Why this night? The World of Outlaws were here, the greatest sprint car drivers on the planet. My dad was in the pits with us. This night seemed to be building up to the perfect opportunity to make myself look like an idiot.

"Oh well, what could go wrong?" I thought.

Unfortunately, my mind went through about a dozen things that could go wrong. The car might not start. I might do something in error and hurt the engine. The throttle could stick. I might not be able to get the car out of gear and run it into the back of the trailer. I've seen it happen. I might forget where our trailer is parked. I might run into one of the Outlaws. It would not be cool to have my ass kicked by Steve Kinser.

Word got around our small team that I was going to start the car.

"Think you can do this, Cool?" (Mr. Cool was a nickname John gave me in high school, which I suspect was given sarcastically) John asked while slapping my back with his skillet-sized hand, sly grin on his face and chuckling to himself.

Dad simply said, "Your mom wouldn't like this," but he was smiling as he said it.

Okay, it was time to take my mind off of this thing. How big of a deal could it be? Actually, I have seen this car starting process turn into a big deal. I've seen cars whose brakes failed run unexpectedly into immovable objects. I've seen them run into other cars. I've seen them run into pedestrians.

I busied myself with my normal anal routine: tightened bolts, made sure the wheels were snug, checked air pressure in the tires, and so on.

Before I knew it other drivers began taking their cars to the starting area. I wanted to back out but Jerry didn't give me the chance. He walked out of the trailer with his helmet and shoved it into my hands. You know you're in trouble when the track requires that you wear a helmet to simply start the car.

"Ready? Let's go," Jerry said without giving me the chance to answer.

I grasped the left side of the roll cage with my left hand, lifted my right leg into the cockpit, and was careful not to crack my head on the wing or the roll cage. I lowered myself into the seat gently, in fear that I might break something. The thought crossed my mind that these cars sail around rough dirt tracks at speeds well over 100 M.P.H. It's highly unlikely I would break something by the simple act of sitting down in the seat.

I had sat in the car at the shop before and the quarters always seemed tight, even though Jerry is a little bigger than I am and the seat fit me loosely. I began feeling slightly claustrophobic and a bit panicky.

I attempted to buckle the five-point harness and quickly realized I didn't know what I was doing. A five-point harness consists of two belts that go over each shoulder, a lap belt, and a submarine belt that comes up between your legs. The five ends all buckle together, hence the name "five-point harness." Earl and Nelson reached in and helped me get it buckled after a few futile attempts at fumbling with it myself. They were also stifling grins.

Dad leaned against the side of the trailer with arms crossed and a smirk on his face. What's up with all the grinning, smiling, and smirking at me? Someone was taking a few snapshots.

I took my hat off and attempted to pull the helmet on my head. I quickly discovered that it is difficult to pull on a helmet while wearing eyeglasses, as they scraped down my nose and dug into my upper lip. I took my glasses off, strapped the helmet on, replaced my glasses through the open visor, and indicated I was ready.

Jerry poked his head in the cockpit and stated, rather than asked, "Are you ready."

I nodded and the crew backed me out of the pit stall. John flagged down a 4-wheeler to push me to the starting area and yelled, "Watch out! Rookie driver!"

An old schoolmate and crewmember of another team, Marty Stephenson, walked by and said, laughing, "Who is that? Todd? Oh, crap!" Very funny.

From that point on everything around me seemed to go silent. Partly because my ears were muffled by the helmet and partly because I was concentrating on the starting process. I noticed that I felt like a little kid sitting in the front seat of a passenger car trying to peer over the dashboard. How the heck do these guys race these things?

The 4-wheeler pushed me (startlingly rapidly, I thought) through the infield and around to the pit lane on the front straight side, and I glanced to my left. There sat the cars and trailers of Steve Kinser, Sammy Swindell, and several other World of Outlaws drivers. All drivers I had watched and admired for years. Just a couple of years ago I sat in the grandstand and only wished I knew somebody in the pits, and now I rode in a sprint car on my way to be pushed off. It was a bit surreal.

I rolled to a stop in the starting area near turn one and turned my head to the right to see one of the track officials motioning a push truck behind me. I looked down and reached for the gear slider with my right hand and set the car in gear. I tried to lean back and forth in the seat to rock the car to make sure it was in gear, which is difficult to do when you're strapped to the seat.

I turned my head again to the official and nodded to indicate I was ready. Here we go. The official gave the push truck driver the thumbs up and I was jerked into motion. These push truck drivers don't mess around. They hit the gas and you sit back in your seat.

Sprint car engines have a fair amount of compression, so it took a moment for the tires to gain traction with the ground and rotate, and start turning the engine. As the engine turned over it gave off a rapid jerking vibration in the car, kind of like driving over a brick road.

I reached for the fuel valve and turned it on, glanced at the oil pressure gauge, and fought to keep the car on the infield starting road between turns one and two. The ride was bouncy and completely awkward. I looked at the oil pressure gauge again and was surprised to see that it was already up past 40 pounds. I kept a death grip on the steering wheel with my right hand, pumped the throttle a couple of times with my right foot, and flipped the mag switch with my left hand to the "on" position.

Whoomph! The engine immediately came to life and my head snapped back into the seat as the car separated from the push truck. The ride instantly became even more jerky and bumpy now that I was under the power of the sprint car. I have seen many drivers give the push truck drivers the cool thumbs up to indicate that their cars were started, but I wasn't about to let go of that steering wheel for the life of me.

I tapped the throttle, for the heck of it, and the car felt like it was going to come out from under me (which I'm sure was imperceptible to anyone who might have been watching). Okay, I won't be doing that again.

The engine was running at a fast idle and it felt like I was picking up speed. I almost panicked when I came to the pit entrance just past turn two because I wasn't sure if I could make the turn. I leaned on the brake pedal, which is located on the left side, with my left foot. Crap. I can't slow it down too much though, or I might kill the dang engine.

To top it off the visor on Jerry's helmet, which was flipped open, somehow became entangled with the head net attached to the right side of the roll cage. The net is there to keep the driver's head within the confines of the roll cage during a crash. In my case it caused me to drive with my head tilted to the right, like a dork.

Luckily I made the turn and headed for our pit stall, which, thank goodness, was a straight shot from the pit entrance that night. "Please God don't let anyone step in front of me," I thought.

I could see our pit stall and everyone waving me in, as if I couldn't see them. One last thing to do - get the car out of gear. I reached down and easily popped it out of gear, and a smug thought of "mission complete" ran through my mind.

Our crew continued to wave me in until they realized I was creeping to a stop about 20 yards short of our pit stall. Oh well, better safe than sorry.

They ran to the car and rolled me into our pit stall. "Well, what did you think?" John asked.

"That was awesome!" I muffled through the helmet.

I shakily took my glasses off and removed the helmet, and suddenly realized how loud it was to sit in between two open headers of a running sprint car. I kind of wanted to sit there and enjoy it for a while. You know, be seen and look cool, like race car drivers do. Maybe put on some sunglasses.

But Jerry leaned into the cockpit and simply said, "Good. Now get out. I've got to get in there and adjust the fuel valve."

I fumbled my way out of the belts, pulled myself from the cockpit, and cracked my head on the wing side panel in the process. I was trembling with excitement and my heart was pounding! Dad was just grinning. I did it! And without any damage!

Jerry quickly brought me back down to earth as he rolled a tire from the trailer and handed me the wheel wrench. "Here," he said, "put this on the right rear and check the air pressure."

Ah, so much for basking in the glory.

Small World

It really is a small world. I know that is a cliché, but clichés stick because they are true.

On race day Saturdays I normally busied myself with household chores that needed to be completed before I left for the races. Doing these chores also helped ease my guilty conscience about leaving the kids behind while I went to have fun later in the day.

One Saturday afternoon I was outside working on my dad's tractor, which I used to mow the yard of the house I rented at the time. The house sat around a quarter of a mile south of County Road F-70, just over the crest of a hill. You could hear traffic on the highway, but couldn't see it.

I was underneath the Woods belly mower of the Case VAC tractor when I heard from the direction of the highway a horn blaring, tires screeching, a disgusting sounding metallic almost explosive impact, and then what I thought sounded like a vehicle flipping down the highway.

I ran to the house and grabbed the cell phone, jumped in the car, and headed for the highway. The wreck sounded so bad, I expected the worst. I didn't know what I would find, or what I would do once I got there.

As I popped over the crest of the hill I couldn't quite believe my eyes. There in the north ditch pointed east-bound was a big white enclosed trailer with a 9H painted on the side.

It was Doran Doty's sprint car hauler. Doran Doty just

happened to be the points leader in the 360 division at Knoxville at the time.

Doran, a former hockey player, was an aggressive, talented, and hard-nosed sprint car driver. I heard that at one point in time he held the record for most penalty minutes while playing for the local USHL Des Moines Buccaneers.

Later in his racing career while driving for car owner Bob Thompson, Thompson quipped, "I don't know if we'll win many races, but I guarantee we won't lose any fights."

I pulled to a stop next to the highway and surveyed the damage. Something just didn't look right. Doran's rig was facing eastbound, but in the north ditch. The other vehicle involved in the accident, a pickup truck, was also facing eastbound, but on the south shoulder.

I walked to the truck and asked the lady therein if she was injured. She said she was all right but had a distressed look on her face. That's understandable. I crossed the highway and walked toward Doran, who was standing next to the front of his truck talking on his cell phone.

I could overhear that instead of speaking with a 911 dispatcher, he was actually trying to contact a tow truck to pull his rig out of the ditch. He blankly looked at me as he spoke on his phone and I don't think he recognized me as one of Jerry's crew guys.

Since I was doing some yard work I was pretty filthy, however I was wearing an old racing hat and Knoxville Raceway jacket. Come to think of it, I probably looked similar to how I looked at the races.

"You okay?" I asked after he got off the phone.

"Yeah," he replied, "Boy, this sort of thing kind of shakes a guy up."

Under the circumstances, the next question I asked I immediately wished I could take back. "Did the race car get hurt?"

But luckily Doran was already talking on the phone again, trying to arrange for a tow truck. The problem was that no tow truck service was willing to come on scene until after the authorities had arrived.

Jeff Morris, a member of Doran's pit crew who I didn't know at the time, had been following Doran in a separate vehicle, towing a boat. Jeff was planning on doing some boating the day after the races, but at the moment he was unhooking the boat trailer from his truck so he could attempt to pull Doran's truck and trailer out of the ditch. He backed up to the front of Doran's truck and tied on with all he had available - a nylon strap normally used to tie down the race car in the trailer. The strap snapped shortly after he began pulling.

Doran's truck and trailer were significantly in the ditch. He had wiped out a reflector post and somehow skated over a large cement culvert. The sprint car remained tied down in the trailer but some spare tires and other items had gotten loose on the inside and took out the nose wing. There was a flat tire on the trailer and the truck sustained quite a bit of sheet metal damage on the right side. But the truck was still running and appeared drivable. The trailer looked to be leaning dangerously toward the downhill side of the ditch, and I stayed clear of that side after my initial inspection to satisfy my curiosity.

I walked back up to Doran and couldn't help but ask, "How'd it happen?"

"I'd been following this lady since Runnells," Doran explained, "and as I came over the crest of the hill she was almost just sitting there at the intersection. I went to pass her on the left side, and she started to turn left. You know how sometimes you see people driving slow trying to find a street or something? That's what it looked like she was doing. I thought I was going to make it, but at the last second she turned. I clipped her left side and the rest is kind of a blur."

Jeff walked over and asked if I lived in the area. I told him I did and he asked if I had a log chain. For some reason I said, "I think so, but I have to find out who borrowed it last." I didn't actually own a log chain but thought my dad had one.

I hopped in the car and headed for my folks' house, which was around two miles away. I ran in the front door of Mom and Dad's, quickly explained the situation, and told them what I was looking for. Evidently I was a bit excited and had to explain the situation again. I finally got my point across and Dad said he had a log chain, but he thought it was over at my sister and brother-in-law's place, which was another two miles away.

"Good grief by the time I find this thing they'll be getting ready to push off for the A feature," I thought to myself.

But once I arrived at my sister and brother-in-law's house I found it pretty quickly in their garage. Luckily they weren't home and I didn't have to try explaining myself again.

I grabbed the log chain and headed back to the accident scene, halfway expecting to see Doran's rig out of the ditch and the local authorities present.

It wasn't, and they weren't.

A neighbor, who had been mushroom hunting when he heard the accident, was attempting to pull the truck and trailer out with his log chain and four-wheel drive truck. It wasn't budging and he was smoking all four tires on the pavement.

"Call Hewitt's and tell them you're the points leader," Jeff told Doran, and Doran got back on the phone.

Hewitt's, located in Monroe, is the wrecker company Knoxville Raceway uses to clear the track when there is an accident and Jeff thought Doran might have a little pull with them. Jeff was right. After the phone call Doran had a tow truck on the way.

Around 15 minutes later the biggest tow truck I have ever seen crested the hill from the east. It was basically a semi-truck with a tow hoist on the back. Once the tow truck arrived and the driver parked it in the proper position, it didn't take long to pull Doran's rig out of the ditch. He simply winched it out.

Shortly thereafter an Iowa State Patrol trooper arrived. He was clearly agitated that they hadn't waited to pull the truck and trailer out of the ditch. He explained that he had been working a fatality on the interstate and that's why it took so long for help to arrive.

The trooper checked on the lady involved in the wreck, found she was feeling some pain, and called for an ambulance.

He then began giving Doran a lecture about, "Everybody's got these cell phones these days and if we had known someone was hurt we would have sent someone immediately."

Of course he was right, but racers tend to have one-track minds. Besides, the lady said she was okay.

I wished Doran better luck for the rest of the night and went back to the house to get ready for the races.

Doran's day didn't improve later at Knoxville. He dropped out of the race program due to mechanical problems, which I don't believe were related to the accident.

Still, it was hard to believe that just a few hours earlier his whole racing outfit was in a ditch only a quarter of a mile away from my house.

I never did mention this incident to Jeff later when he helped with Jerry's racing operation, and I don't think he recognized me from that day.

But like I said, small world.

"Just Pull it in After the Green"

In January of 1999, Jerry, as he was often known to do, raced in a flat track indoor motorcycle race in northeastern Iowa. He simply could not stay away from racing during the sprint car off-season.

While racing through a corner at the tight racetrack he pulled along the inside of another bike in an attempt to make a pass. Unfortunately, Jerry's right leg made contact with the other rider's rear tire and Jerry took a nasty spill. He was 55 years old at the time.

His right leg was hurting significantly, but that wasn't the real problem. The injury to his right leg caused him to favor it with his left leg, which was his bad one. Jerry had raced motorcycles, 3-wheelers, 4-wheelers - you name it - since the '60's. During that time he had damaged his left knee more than he knew, or at least let on.

Well, favoring his right leg with his left leg began causing big-time problems with his left knee. Being the stubborn old racer that he is, he didn't go to the doctor. He simply tried to get by and tough it out. The knee swelled up to twice its normal size and you could see it through his blue jeans. You could tell by the look on his face that he was in a great deal of pain, although he never complained.

The sprint car season was well underway before he finally kept an appointment with the doctor. The doctor's prognosis was not good: bone spurs, no cartilage, arthritis, and bone-on-bone. It would never heal if left alone and knee replacement surgery was needed.

Jerry did not like this, but the pain was too great and he knew he needed the surgery. Worst of all he couldn't get around like he was accustomed. He could barely walk, or climb into the sprint car. Each time he sat in the car it was like a new experience in pain. He didn't notice it so much when the green flag was flying, but the pace laps were unbearable.

He made the decision that made me realize how much pain he must have been in - he would have the surgery during the season.

To no one's surprise, he procrastinated. He was making attempts to run in the 410 class and there were big upcoming races. The Master's Classic, his sprint car claim to fame, was coming up in a few weeks and the 360 Nationals was after that. No, he couldn't have the surgery just yet because he had racing to do. He talked the chief surgeon at the Veteran's Hospital in Des Moines into postponing the surgery and scheduled it for Monday, June 14, two days after the 360 Nationals.

He made it through the Master's Classic and turned in a fifth-place finish in someone else's car (which he thought was faster than his own). The next weekend was the three-day 360 Nationals and he decided to qualify on Thursday night of the event.

Normally he never called to ask for my help. When I got home from work that Thursday and found out he called wondering if I would be at Knoxville, I knew he must have been in desperate need of assistance. Since it was a work night, and I was getting wimpier as the years rolled by, I hadn't planned on helping that night. But since he called I figured I better get my butt to Knoxville.

It rained prior to the race and more rain was threatening, so track officials decided to pit all the cars in the livestock barns on the Marion County Fairgrounds, just off the fourth turn of the racetrack. In my experience every time we pitted in the barns due to potential rain, we ended up getting rained out. Such was the case this night, although they did manage to run a few time trials.

We tried again the next night with the same routine, pitting in the barns. Once again, a rain out. Although we did get enough of the racing program in to set a lineup for the Saturday night finals of the Nationals. Jerry would start in the middle of the pack of the C feature.

When I arrived in Knoxville Saturday night it was clear that something was wrong with Jerry.

A combination of two days racing and walking on the uneven ground in the pits on Saturday made his knee really act up. They had us unload and take the trailer outside the track, which only added more stress to his knee. It was the worst I had seen it and he couldn't walk without assistance.

We discussed whether Jerry should race that night, and he decided he would not. Starting in the middle of the C and knee replacement surgery on Monday, it just wasn't worth it.

That was all Jan needed to hear and she began making plans to load up before the races would start. It was too late to pull the trailer back into the pits to load the car and equipment, so she pondered which items she could carry out herself.

The first thing she took out was Jerry's helmet and driving suit. She knows Jerry all too well.

Jerry and I commandeered a little 4-wheeler from another racer's crew and took three jugs of fuel to the trailer. Riding back through the backstretch pit gate track officials advised they wouldn't allow us to haul any more equipment out of the pits until after the races. This worried Jan because she knew that once they started warming up those engines, Jerry would want to race.

Of course, she was correct.

"Where's my helmet and driving suit?" Jerry barked at Jan.

"I took it out to the trailer," Jan barked back. "You don't need it, you're not racing."

You could see the wheels turning in Jerry's head. He was calculating a logical reason to race.

"Go find out what we get paid if we don't start," he told Jan.

Jan, hoping against hope that she would receive the answer she wanted to hear, ran off with her clipboard showing the line-up and found an official. She came back shortly with a frown on her face, knowing what Jerry would say. She told him that the car would need to start the race for him to be paid.

After a brief little discussion between the two of them

consisting of, "Go get my helmet and driving suit," and, "No I'm not going to go get your helmet and driving suit," Jan finally gave in. (Jerry asked me to go get it at one point, to which I replied, "No way, I'm staying out of this one.")

Jerry said he would take the green flag and then pull the car into the pits. Jan and I looked at each other doubtfully. I think she was grasping to the slight chance that Jerry would do this.

Jerry handed me his helmet and ordered, "Go start the car."

I wasn't expecting this and gave him my "you need to give me a week's notice so I can prepare myself" speech, to no avail.

To make an embarrassing story short, it took me three attempts to get that damn thing started. The first time it didn't even fire. I really don't know what happened. The second time it started, but was idling too fast and I didn't think I was going to make the turn back into the pits. I had to pop it out of gear to make the turn, and it died shortly thereafter. The third time was the charm and it stayed running, and I coasted back into our pit stall.

"What happened?" Jerry asked.

I gave him my "you need to give me a week's notice" speech again, once more to no avail. I decided to never speak of the incident again. Thankfully not long thereafter the track required the driver to wear a fire suit to start a car, which put an end to my car starting days.

Since Jerry was going to "just pull it in after the green" we had not completed any work on the car to set it up for track conditions that night. It was still set up for the dry slick track that existed before the rain out of the previous evening. On this night it was totally opposite, a much heavier track. Even though Jerry said he would pull the car in immediately after the start of the race, I stood by the car and fretted. I knew Jerry. A car set up for a dry slick track could spell trouble on a heavy tacky track.

He had me make some changes to loosen up the car not long before he was scheduled to race. This relieved me but also confirmed my suspicion that he was probably not going to "just pull it in after the green."

Jerry started 10th and finished seventh, in one of the gutsiest performances I've seen. While that may not sound great, considering the amount of pain he was experiencing, I was mightily impressed. He's a tough old boot.

Dennis Moore, Jr. won both the 360 Nationals A main feature and the 410 feature that night.

Jerry pulled into our pit stall after his race and I could tell he was relieved it was over. Jan was very relieved.

After the races Jan cooked us hamburgers and hotdogs on an open grill in the pits, because she figured with Jerry's surgery in two days it might be a while before we raced at Knoxville again.

This was somewhat true. The surgery went off without complications and the next race he participated in was on July 17. Pretty remarkable considering that knee replacement surgery at the time basically consisted of sawing the knee off and replacing it with something that really isn't supposed to be in the human body.

We ate and bench-raced, and Jerry took in the accolades and wishes of good luck for his surgery from fellow racers, crew members, friends, and fans.

As I sat and relaxed, I turned to Jerry and said, "Just pull it in after the green. Yeah. Right. You'll never do that."

Jerry got a good laugh out of that.

High Jinks

Sprint car drivers tend to be, by nature, a bit ornery. I don't know if it coincides with the part of their brains that make them strap into a sprint car and plant the throttle to the floor with apparent complete disregard for personal safety or not, but they do seem to have a penchant for mischief.

I witnessed this characteristic firsthand one year at a benefit dinner for the Marion County Chapter of the American Heart Association. This is one of those dinners where you are served by celebrities, in this case sprint car drivers, and you have to tip them for everything they do. There was a competition to see which driver could accumulate the most tips, and all tips gathered throughout the night were then donated to the American Heart Association.

Here's how it works: when they bring you silverware, you tip them; when they bring you water, you tip them; when they steal the butter from your table, you tip them to get it back. I witnessed more than one diner learn the lesson that you should not leave any money lying on the table, as the drivers would walk by and snatch it away as an easy tip.

Jerry was one of the servers that night and brought a secret weapon to use just in case he was behind on tips and needed to make up ground. He disappeared for a few minutes and then emerged wearing a sports bra stuffed with socks, much to the delight of everyone in attendance.

Jan, who had helped Jerry squeeze into the bra, went to the

announcer and whispered something into his ear.

Giggling, the announcer called everyone to attention over the microphone and said, "Jerry, it's the driver that has the most TIPS! TIPS, Jerry, TIPS!"

After the dinner they held an auction for racing memorabilia, with the proceeds going to the American Heart Association. Items included racing photos, t-shirts, quilts, helmets, and many other race-related items. All were donated by race car drivers, teams, businesses, and organizations in the community.

At one point they started auctioning off several racing t-shirts at once at the bidder's choice. This meant the highest bidder bought his choice of shirt, second highest bidder bought second choice, etc.

I was leaning back in my chair, minding my own business, and enjoying the evening with my arm rested over the back of the chair next to me. The auctioneer had the bids for the shirts up to $17.50.

The next thing I knew my arm was involuntarily raised in the air, the auctioneer pointed directly at me and yelled, "Sold!" and I had bought myself a Scott "Breezy" Whitworth t-shirt.

Jaymie Moyle, a native of Australia who has raced and worked in the United States for several years, had walked by and hoisted my arm in the air, apparently thinking I looked like I needed a new t-shirt.

"Thanks for your support," he said in his Australian accent, grinning from ear to ear.

He repeated this little trick on others several times throughout the night. After that incident I learned my lesson and kept my arms firmly planted by my sides.

Later in the evening Jerry signed his sports bra and it was auctioned off for $30 - which is, in and of itself, a bit disturbing.

High jinks aren't solely reserved for drivers. One night there was a guy in the pits at Knoxville who was apparently involved with IndyCar racing in some fashion. He was a friend-of-a-friend-of-a-friend of someone, and he along with another guy stopped by our pit stall.

We got the impression that the IndyCar guy kind of looked

down his nose at and sort of pooh-poohed dirt track sprint car racing. Everything was IndyCar this, and IndyCar that. He seemed just a tad snooty. The type of person who might lift his pinky finger while drinking a cup of tea.

Now, I can appreciate almost any form of racing, but this guy rubbed us the wrong way. After all, we were sprint car people. We believed in the old adage that dirt is for racing and pavement is for getting to the track.

Anyway, we kind of started poking fun at this guy behind his back.

Going back and forth with our somewhat mean-spirited fun-making, at one point I said in a "la-di-da" fashion, "Well, if you think IndyCar is so great, I won a race at the Go-Cart Ranch in Okoboji last week."

This was only an exaggeration, because I did feel like Steve Kinser the previous week during our annual Okoboji vacation. I felt like him while putting a hurting on my brother-in-law, niece, nephew, and son on the slick track that once existed at the Ranch amusement park in the Iowa Great Lakes. (I accomplished this by keeping the cart straight in the corners, maintained momentum by letting it feed wide on the straights, running inches from the wall. Even the teenage kid working the track hopped in a cart and couldn't catch me.)

Jan and Tracie thought this comment was funny. So much so that the next week they brought me a custom-made t-shirt which read, "Okoboji Go-Cart Champ."

I've never worn the shirt, but I still have it. I should probably hang it up in the man cave someday.

One year following the Knoxville season finale Lee Nelson's wife at the time talked me into wearing a sports bra after the races. I guess more accurately, Jerry talked me into wearing it.

Lucy Detrick left the bra in our trailer for me with a note saying I was out of uniform. Lucy is Mark Detrick's wife and they own Detrick Excavating, who was one of our sponsors. She left the note because the ladies on our crew preferred to wear these sports bras as normal outerwear to the races every week, at least on the warm nights. Lucy felt I should conform to the dress code.

Lee's wife said she would try on the bra if I did.

Not one to miss a free show of parts of the female anatomy, Jerry leaned in and said to me, "Come on, if you put it on then we get to watch her put it on."

I held up my end of the bargain, but much to our disappointment she simply pulled the bra over the top of the shirt she was wearing.

They made me pose in such a way as to show cleavage. Unfortunately there are pictures of me wearing that thing that I hope to someday find and destroy.

One of the most bizarre things I ever witnessed occurred after the season finale race at the Iowa State Fairgrounds one year. As usual a few of the race teams were hanging around after the races, drinking a few adult beverages, and enjoying themselves. One racer, let's call him, oh, I don't know, "Fred," and his pit crew were celebrating the birthday of one of their crew members.

After most of the fans and other race teams left for the night, a stripper appeared out of nowhere to dance for the birthday boy. The stripper started her routine and a small crowd immediately gathered to watch the proceedings. The stripper went through the process of taking off her clothes, piece by piece, much to the amusement of the crowd. Since this was a public place I thought the stripper would surely only strip down to a G-string or bikini, or something akin to a PG-13 rating.

I was wrong.

The stripper did strip down to a G-string, but then removed her top. This very much pleased the mostly male crowd. The poor birthday boy, by this time seated on a chair in "Fred's" enclosed trailer with the stripper dancing all around him, was extremely red-faced.

One thing led to another and the striptease advanced to the point where the crowd was now trying to convince the birthday boy to remove his clothes. That was when I began rethinking the life choices I had made which led me to that point.

The crowd did manage to pressure the birthday boy into at least dropping his pants, but thankfully not his underwear, much to their delight. But that wasn't quite good enough for

"Fred." I still have a hard time believing what followed.

"Fred" emerged from the crowd, made his way into the trailer, and started taking off his clothes. Unfortunately he did not stop at his underwear. The stripper also did not stop at taking off her top.

The next thing I knew, "Fred" and the stripper were walking hand in hand buck naked through the pits at the Iowa State Fairgrounds. At one point they walked to Jerry's sprint car still parked in the pits, and began inspecting it. I was relieved that they did not touch the car.

The next night at Knoxville another driver's girlfriend walked by "Fred," looked him up and down as if she didn't know him, and said, "'Fred!' I'm sorry, I didn't recognize you with your clothes on!"

Nationals

Knoxville is a special place on a weekly basis, but it transforms itself into something else during the Knoxville Nationals. It is a true "gathering of the clans," as they say. It is the place to be for four days in August if you have anything to do with sprint car racing.

Fans from all over the world make the pilgrimage to this small Iowa town, nearly tripling its size, and have spent millions of their hard-earned dollars in the south-central part of the state. Friendships are made there that last a lifetime, sometimes renewing them only at that time of year.

Once you walk onto the Marion County Fairgrounds during the Nationals, the colors seem brighter, the sounds crisper, and there is a definite feel of electricity in the air.

I always felt like a kid on Christmas Eve the night before the Nationals. I'd take vacation the four days, sometimes the entire week, for the sprint car festival. And that's really what it is, with vendors from all over the country there to promote and sell their wares, a trade show, in the past a driver softball game, parade, auctions, food stands, t-shirt stands, golf tournament, and a multitude of other things to do during the week. Area hotels and campgrounds are full.

Many of the traveling drivers and race teams enjoy the Nationals simply because it's one of the few times during the season where they can spend four days in a row in one place.

It is the biggest race of the year in sprint car racing, bar none, and is considered the sport's version of the Indianapolis 500 or Daytona 500. It is the crown jewel and every sprint car driver in the world dreams of winning this race. Danny Lasoski once said he really didn't care how much it paid to win, which now is up to $150,000, but that he really just wanted that Knoxville Nationals trophy. Seasons are made or lost during those four days in August.

It has changed over the years though. Gone are the skin-to-win wet t-shirt contests, campers parked in rows directly behind the main grandstand, and (before my time) poker games where race cars have been won and lost. But for me those four days in August generated some of my fondest memories about racing.

I remember parking my dad's old Suburban, multi-colored from primer due to body work that my brother-in-law never quite got around to completing, outside of the fourth turn fence one year. John, my cousin, and I decided to park it there on Friday of the Nationals and camp out for the night.

We stayed up too late and awoke the next morning to the swaying of the Suburban. Through blurry eyes I was startled to see the smiling bearded face of Ted Hulgan through the left rear side window, rocking the vehicle back and forth.

"Time for breakfast," he barked at us.

I'm pretty sure he scared the crap out of my cousin, who was all of about 13 at the time. I think we corrupted that poor kid.

Ted is a character in his own right. A scruffy, tattooed guy, he looks like he just dismounted his Harley after arriving in Sturgis. But as with other biker-types I've met he is one of the nicest guys you'll ever meet, if you're on his good side. I got to know Ted through my brother-in-law, who was a grade school through high school classmate of Ted's. Ted had attended the races more years than he can remember, later crewed on a 410 sprint car team, and even later served as a push truck driver.

We all hopped into his topless Blazer and headed to Hardee's for breakfast. It was around 7:00 a.m. and I was not too surprised to see a few people around the fairgrounds who apparently were still partying from the night before. You could always find a party during the Nationals at any time of day.

We drove by the legendary Dingus Lounge, and I was glad to see it was still standing and had survived another night of the Nationals. I don't know if the same could be said about its patrons. For some reason I can count on one hand the number of times I've visited that famous place, which seems like a missed opportunity, especially since it sits across the street from the track. I guess I just didn't like leaving Marion County Fairgrounds property.

During the rain-plagued 1987 Nationals, the year they ran three days of racing on Saturday, I bought a pit pass for the first time and watched one of the postponed qualifying features standing on a giant dirt mound near turn four. The mound was created by the track maintenance crew when they scraped the layer of mud from the infield and piled it in that spot. The dirt mound attracted several infield spectators as it offered a better view from a precarious perch a few feet above the ground.

It was from that perch where I got a good chuckle watching John walk alongside Bobby Allen, trying to strike up a conversation with him, until John slipped in the mud and did a neat little jig to keep his balance, which also caused a good chuckle out of Mr. Allen. Later that afternoon I took a nap on the infield grass while time trials were completed for the other postponed qualifying night.

We went back to our grandstand seats for the finals and they didn't get the D feature pushed off until midnight. Earlier in the night my poor dad, who came only for the finals, had beer spilled all over him by a drunken race reveler sitting behind us.

That may have been the year that some fans began dumpster diving in an attempt to amuse themselves during one of the rain delays. They would jump from the front of the stands into a dumpster directly below. Officials didn't allow that to last too long, but my dad talked about viewing that activity for years.

I'm not sure when the checkered flag fell on the A feature but I remember the sky was starting to lighten a bit when we got home. Steve Kinser added another Knoxville Nationals title to his name that year.

During the 1988 Nationals John and I attended a benefit auction for Brad Doty, a World of Outlaws driver who was paralyzed in an accident at The Kings Royal in Rossburg, Ohio, just a few weeks prior.

The auction was held one afternoon in the grandstand on one of those 110-degrees-in-the-shade kind of days. We were kept entertained and distracted from the heat by watching the legendary J.W. Hunt win the bid on an item, return the item, and then win the bid on the same item, multiple times.

I came home with a Brad Doty print signed by Greg Wooley, Kenny Jacobs, Cris Eash, Danny Smith, and future Knoxville Nationals champions Bobby Allen, Dave Blaney, and Danny Lasoski. It remains the centerpiece of my racing memorabilia collection. Steve Kinser won the Nationals that year, once again.

Another year we took part in the golf tournament held during the Nationals. As we hung out on the deck of the country club at Pine Knolls Golf Course in Knoxville, waiting to start our round, none other than Steve Kinser, Danny Lasoski, and World of Outlaws founder Ted Johnson came strolling up to the clubhouse.

Lasoski was a bundle of energy, talking a mile a minute and pulling the pockets of his shorts inside out to prove to Ted that he didn't have any money and needed to be given some in order to partake in the event. Ted simply rolled his eyes as the two entered the clubhouse, while Lasoski continued to chatter in his ear. The look on Ted's face made me think he had heard this type of conversation before.

Kinser, on the other hand, was totally relaxed as he leaned on the deck railing right next to us and struck up a casual conversation. He asked how they run the tournament and we explained the shotgun start. He told us how they run the tournament at the Indianapolis Motor Speedway, and about the holes in the infield at that famous track.

In other words, he acted like any other regular guy. This was a far cry from the focused, intimidating figure we were accustomed to seeing at the racetrack.

As our conversation continued with this uncharacteristically relaxed Steve Kinser, Lasoski emerged from the clubhouse carrying a couple of cans of pop (what we call a carbonated soft drink in Iowa). A mischievous grin appeared on his face as he winked at us and nonchalantly lingered unnoticed a few steps behind Kinser, who was still leaning against the railing and gazing out over the golf course.

All of us, except Kinser, realized Lasoski was up to something. He then began vigorously shaking one of the cans of pop.

After more than a sufficient amount of shaking, Lasoski casually walked up to Kinser and handed him the shaken can of pop.

Straight-faced he said, "Here, Steve," and took a couple steps back.

Unbeknownst to Steve, the half-dozen or so of us hanging out there all stood and held our breath, intensely watching the can and inching away from what was sure to come.

Kinser took the can and reached for the pull-tab.

The rest of us tensed up and prepared for the inevitable.

He popped the can open and...

Absolutely nothing happened.

It was amazing. We stood there in stunned silence with surprised looks of confusion and disbelief on our faces as Kinser, oblivious to what Lasoski tried to do, took a swig of pop.

Lasoski's shoulders drooped noticeably in disappointment and the smile left his face. Steve Kinser regularly caused this sort of reaction in other drivers with his on-track performances, and apparently this invulnerability carries over to his regular everyday life.

That was the moment when I realized this legend truly does have some sort of supernatural powers over the laws of physics. Steve Kinser added another Knoxville Nationals title to his name that year. I believe this happened in either 1991 or 1992, but it doesn't matter - he won them both.

For a few years John, Brad, Smooth, and I held tickets to sit in the grandstand. I always liked to take my seat early to watch hot laps and time trials. In all honesty, at the time I probably would have paid to watch a sprint car stand still.

John, on the other hand, thoroughly despised sitting through time trials. So normally he would hang out at an acquaintance's campsite outside the track, prepping himself for the night via adult beverages.

By the time heat races were set to begin, John was primed and ready to go. One night, as the first heat race prepared to push off, John came strolling up the aisle with a 32-ounce beer in one hand, enormous stogie protruding from the corner of his mouth, ball cap tilted on the top of his bushy blonde head, and a big grin on his face. To top it off he was wearing shorts that all four of us purchased that week which were white and displayed large black outlines of sprint cars printed all the way around them. We were all wearing them that night and surely we looked like a bunch of goofballs. Brad laughed and had to point him out, just to make sure we could appreciate viewing John in all his glory.

Anyway, it took John a while to make his way to his seat because he was stopped several times by other fans in our vicinity. He had gotten to know these fans over the years, since most folks opted to purchase the same seats each year unless they could upgrade to seats higher in the grandstand.

He flopped down in his seat and the heat races began. At that time it was an annual tradition for fans to bring beach balls to bat around in between races to pass time. It was kind of a fun diversion to watch the beach balls bounce around, and almost an honor if you were actually able to take a whack at one.

John had sort of an obsession about hitting one of those beach balls over the back of the grandstand (before the suites were added). It would have been tough to do from where we sat at the time, which was a little over halfway to the top. But John is a big guy and if anyone could do it, it would probably be him. He came close a few times, and was always on the lookout for the perfect opportunity.

On this night the opportunity presented itself. In between races, as he stood and talked to fans in the row behind ours, a beach ball bounded directly towards him. With a grin on his face he stopped his conversation in mid-sentence, caught the ball with one hand, and placed his beer on the seat.

His eagle eyes squinted as he focused on the top of the grandstand. Then, in a move reminiscent of a volleyball server, he tossed the ball up and drew his skillet-sized hand way back behind his head.

WHACK!

Maybe it was the pre-race beverages, or maybe his trajectory was just off, but immediately after his hand made contact with the beach ball it shot like a line drive smack-dab into the face of a middle-aged woman four rows behind ours.

An audible gasp came from many fans around us, as we all turned away and unsuccessfully tried to stifle the giggles. John hunched his shoulders, muttered a "sorry about that" to the lady, quickly turned around, and sat down.

Trying not to laugh himself he turned to us and said, "Did you see that?"

Of course, we had.

A couple of weeks later a letter to the editor appeared in *National Speed Sport News* from a lady who wrote to complain about the beach balls at the Knoxville Nationals. She only mentioned that they were a nuisance and distraction, but I like to think the letter was written by the lady whose face John smashed with the beach ball.

In another example of getting to know the folks you sit next to during Nationals, for a few years we sat near the nicest couple who traveled to Knoxville from the far northwest corner of the country. We got to know them better after they mentioned several times how much I looked like their son, who hadn't made the trip.

The next year they brought and showed us several photos of their son taken from different angles - and honestly, the resemblance was uncanny. So much so that Jim Harris jokingly asked if my dad was ever stationed in the northwest part of the country when he was in the service, and if he served around the time their son was born (not possible, Dad served in the 50's).

The couple owned a Christmas tree farm and one year mailed me a four-foot tree over the holidays. That was awesome, and those are the types of people you meet at the Nationals.

It was during the Nationals one year that John and I talked to Jeff Gordon in the old restroom/dressing room that was once located in the middle of the infield. (I embellish, as my part of the conversation mostly consisted of me grinning and nodding my head like an idiot.) John asked Jeff about an incident we had watched recently on the ESPN *Thursday Night Thunder* broadcast.

In that midget race Jeff was racing against the legendary Rich Vogler and the two got together, sending Jeff to the infield with a broken race car. Clearly upset after unbuckling and climbing from his car, Jeff raised his arms in a "What the heck was that?" fashion towards Vogler as the field passed by him under caution.

But when we talked to him Jeff took the diplomatic route and claimed it to be just a racing incident. Jeff was in the process of changing out of his driving suit and stood in his fireproof long underwear as he spoke to us. When I tell people we talked to Jeff Gordon while he was only in his underwear I usually receive a bewildered facial expression in return.

I recall the first race Gordon competed in at Knoxville. It happened in 1987 and was big news because he was only 15 years old at the time. He was fast in Bob Trostle's second car, but became entangled with another on the front stretch during the A feature.

I have a copy of the next week's Knoxville Raceway program and it shows a picture of his car piled up with the other, however there is no photo caption. But on one of the cars you can barely see Trostle's signature #20 on top of the wing in the glare of the lights, and the added "X" on the side panel indicating the second car. It was not surprising to see how Gordon's NASCAR success exploded following his sprint car days.

Through all the years I attended races at Knoxville I only had one brief conversation with then future Hall of Famer Terry McCarl. It occurred during a Knoxville Nationals one year while I watched the races in the infield near turn three from the box of John's pickup truck.

Pickup trucks regularly attract drivers, since they offer a better vantage point a few feet above the ground. On that night Terry walked up and asked if he could come aboard.

I of course said, "Absolutely."

He reached for the tailgate and prepared to climb up, but paused for a moment.

He then said, "This looks like a plumber's truck."

He was able to quickly deduce this because the box of John's pickup was crammed with copper, PVC pipe, and other fittings commonly used in the plumbing trade.

I laughed and said, "Yup," and Terry climbed on up.

Knoxville had recently changed some of the qualifying procedures and I asked what he thought about them. He simply replied that it didn't matter much to him since they were the same for everyone.

Coincidentally, several years later I had the opportunity to watch Terry's son Austin play in several basketball games for Southeast Polk High School. This is because his son and my son attended that school, and my son played drums in the pep band for all the doubleheader home games.

Austin was a hard-nosed star player for the team. I got the chance to watch him compete against future NBA player Harrison Barnes, once at a home game, and then again in the state finals. Austin showed absolutely no fear going up against the future NBA star.

I theorized this was because throughout his life he observed his father compete with the best sprint car drivers in the world and regularly experience a great deal of success against them. Confidence like that is bound to pass down from generation to generation.

I occasionally see Terry at the Hy-Vee grocery store in Altoona, getting groceries, just like I'm doing. That always seems a bit surreal to me.

After the Thursday night rain cancellation during the 2005 Nationals, I was pretty proud of myself that I had thought to bring an umbrella and remained fairly dry in the pits. After the show was postponed I walked on the sidewalk the few blocks south of the track to my parking spot hosted by the Knoxville High School baseball team.

Strolling along and minding my own business, I glanced to my left and noticed water pooling on the road next to the curb.

About the time I thought, "I'm sure glad cars are staying away from those puddles," I was blasted by a sheet of water generated from a passing truck driving through the standing liquid.

I'm pretty sure it looked like what you may have seen on YouTube videos. I'm guessing anyone behind me got a good chuckle out of the sight, unless they had suffered the same fate. I said a few curse words and continued walking to my car, trying to appear unfazed.

I think it was a push truck from the track and probably done on purpose. Those guys can be ornery.

If I had to name a favorite Nationals I'd probably have to go with 1990, the year Bobby Allen won. Allen ran his patented low line and battled Sammy Swindell over the final several laps of the A feature. Sammy ran the top in his smoking mount, which was covering him in oil. That was also the year Wolfgang finished fifth in the A, running the alphabet after starting the night in the D feature.

Allen stayed at the track long after the checkereds fell, signing autographs and greeting fans who were ecstatic with the upset win. I was giddy after giving him a congratulatory handshake outside the pit gate before I went home that night.

My least favorite was in 1998, when Jerry attempted to qualify on Thursday night of the Nationals and didn't make it out of a last chance heat race. Once we were done for the night I crossed the track and watched the rest of the night's races in the stands with my dad.

Jerry didn't race the Friday non-qualifier program so Dad and I watched again from the stands. I always enjoyed our pre-race ritual of eating at the McDonald's on the south edge of town, enjoying the sprint car photos that adorned the walls at the time. Walking to the car after the races we got caught in a rain shower and had to hustle back to where we were parked in the field southwest of the track.

The next afternoon I received a call saying my dad wasn't feeling well and an ambulance had been summoned. Once at the hospital we found out he had suffered his second heart attack in six years. I missed my first Nationals final since I started attending in 1985, but that was the least of my worries.

Danny Lasoski won his first Nationals championship that year, and I still have an unused ticket for that night's event. Thankfully Dad survived his second open heart surgery the following week.

One thing I always liked to do during Nationals was watch the trophy presentation for the A feature winner. It's great during a regular Saturday night show, but at the Nationals it is where you can see what this race really means to these drivers.

It is uninhibited, pure celebration. Back then if you held a crew card you were able to gain admittance to the pits for the same price as a weekly show, which allowed an up-close view of the proceedings.

Between 1985 and 2005 I had only watched Doug Wolfgang, Steve Kinser, Bobby Allen, Mark Kinser, Dave Blaney, Danny Lasoski, and Kraig Kinser win this race. All were extremely excited and animated when celebrating their wins.

In a Rob Gray written *Des Moines Register* article during the rain-plagued 2005 Knoxville Nationals, Terry McCarl was quoted saying, "Knoxville has such an aura about it. It really isn't about the money - the money's nice on Monday morning... But what winning Nationals does is immortalize you in our sport."

That feeling was displayed the same year when Steve Kinser's 20-year-old son Kraig won the Knoxville Nationals. After coming from the 17th starting spot to finish 7th, I watched from the infield as Steve Kinser took two cool down laps, continuously pumping his fist in celebration of his son's first Nationals win.

After pulling into his pit stall Steve unbuckled, climbed out of the cockpit, and threw his helmet about 30 feet in the air. He then ran to the front stretch and gave his son a bear hug, right before Kraig climbed the catch fence to celebrate, much to the delight of the fans. I can only imagine the joy Kraig felt, winning the race he had watched his father dominate so many years.

In stark contrast, on the day after the Nationals, Knoxville almost seems like a ghost town.

One year after deciding to camp overnight after the final race I awoke to rainy skies and an almost empty campground, which at the time was just west of the track. I kind of expected to see a tumbleweed blow by as I scanned the fairgrounds. It was depressing.

I think you can gauge how great an occasion is by how great the feeling of melancholy is when it's over. Post-Nationals always produced a large amount of melancholy for me.

A Dream Comes True

Two weeks prior to the 1998 Masters Classic, Jerry's engine threw a rod through the block and oil pan. This was a bigger problem than normal because The Masters was a race Jerry had experienced some success at in the past. He finished second in the inaugural event in 1993, and third the previous year. This was a race Jerry always had a chance at winning, and if he was going to win a race at Knoxville he needed to do it soon. At nearly 55 years of age and counting, he was rapidly running out of time.

The Masters was an annual 360 race for drivers 50 years old and older held at Knoxville Raceway on Hall of Fame induction weekend. But this was no easy race to win. Jerry would have to go up against some of the legends of sprint car racing: John Bankston, former track champion Mike Brooks, Cliff "Woody" Woodward, Indy 500 participant Billy Engelhart, 1990 Knoxville Nationals Champion "Scruffy" Bobby Allen, "The Ohio Traveler" Rick Ferkel, Jon Backlund, Edd French, and many others.

Car counts for this event averaged nearly 28 cars from 1993 to 1998. Some skepticism existed when this race was originally conceived, but believe me - none of these guys ever forgot how to stand on the loud pedal of a sprint car.

Not having the funds or time to fix his current or buy a new engine, Jerry burned up his phone lines in an attempt to borrow a powerplant. He was eventually successful and made arrangements to rent another driver's engine for the event. The rent would be a percentage of whatever Jerry earned for his finish in the race.

For this race Jerry had to run time trials, which was somewhat of a rarity for us since we normally drew for heat race starting positions. He was the twelfth driver to qualify and timed in ninth at 17.786 seconds, which was not bad for a 360 cubic inch engine at Knoxville at the time. John Bankston set quick-time with a lap of 17.011 seconds.

Jerry started on the inside of the third row in the first of three seven lap heat races. Dave Farren, Sr., Shelby Steenson, Earnest Jennings, and Chris Maurer started in front of him. Lloyd Armey was on the outside of Jerry, with Wayne Reutimann and John Bankston starting behind. Roy Jo Peltz was a DNS (did not start).

At the drop of the green flag Jerry entered low in turn one in sixth place and drifted up near the cushion in the middle of the track between turns one and two. He went back to the bottom, got a great run coming out of turn two, and made it three wide going down the back chute.

When three cars attempt to enter a corner side by side, sometimes three do not exit. Such was the case this time as the right front wheel of Earnest Jennings, the middle car in the three-wide sandwich, got in front of the left rear of Lloyd Armey's car on the outside.

The rear of Armey's car hopped up in the air, but came back down and he kept running. Jennings' car, on the other hand, made a sudden right turn – never a good thing in a counter-clockwise race – and went headlong into the fence just before the signal light in turn three. His car spun around and did sort of a side roll and came to rest on its right side, junking it and causing the first red flag of the night.

You can't say these guys didn't come to race.

Officials called for a complete restart since the red flag occurred on the first lap. Jerry restarted in third right behind Farren, with Steenson on the outside of the front row. He stayed on the bottom entering turn one, Farren slid up the track, and Jerry went by on the inside and moved to second place coming out of turn two.

Jerry kept to the bottom going into turn three and executed a smooth and fairly polite slide job on the outside running Steenson in turn four. A slide job occurs when a driver follows a car into a corner, dives to the bottom, and attempts to slide up in front of the other driver coming out of the turn.

Oftentimes at some point during a slide job one of the two drivers involved needs to make a decision regarding whether or not to check up, otherwise something bad will happen. I'd say this slide job was fairly polite because it appeared that neither Steenson nor Jerry had to check up. Jerry passed the flag stand and officially led the first full green flag lap.

He led until the yellow flag flew on the third lap, after the cars of Armey and Maurer became entangled on the front stretch. Both cars ended up next to the inside guardrail with Armey's car bouncing to a stop facing the wrong direction, yet stayed upright.

Races were restarted on the backstretch at the time. An orange construction cone was tied to a rope and placed on the track. The leader started the race and the cars that followed couldn't pass another car until they went by the cone on the outside. Once all cars passed the cone a track official dragged it back to the infield by pulling on the rope.

On the restart Jerry went to the cushion and stretched it out, ran and hid, and won by a straightway.

As former track announcer Tim Trier used to say, "He had the wick turned up and the kite string out!"

Following Jerry at the finish line were Steenson, Reutimann, Armey, Farren, Maurer, and Bankston in an ill-running car (Bankston also ran his 410 in the accompanying All Star Circuit of Champions show that night). Due to his earlier crash Jennings was scored eighth, and the DNS of Roy Jo Peltz was ninth.

Mike Brooks won the second heat after starting in eighth, and Edd French in the #7777 won the third heat after starting in sixth.

I would need to defer to Jan to explain how the lineup was determined for the A feature. Jerry was set to start 10th, French 9th, and Brooks 3rd. It must have had something to do with passing points, time trials, a dartboard, or some other game of chance.

The race was going to be a challenge for Jerry coming from that far back in the field, especially with names like Brooks, Bankston, and Engelhart starting in front of him. But one advantage went to Jerry, and that was the 22 lap length of the race. He was in better shape physically than many of the drivers half his age who he normally raced against.

The green flag waved for the feature and Jerry followed Chuck Graves into turn one. Graves jumped the cushion and had a little "oh crap" moment as he gathered it in and regained control. This allowed Jerry to go by on the inside of Graves in turn two, with his right rear tire just below the berm.

Jerry stayed on the high side throughout the lap and entered turn one of the second lap in ninth. He went three wide, tip-toed around the top carrying momentum, and came out of turn two in seventh.

By the time he crossed the line for the start of the fourth lap Jerry had moved up to sixth. Then the red flag came out after Larry Hansen rolled in turn four.

We all rushed to Jerry's car in the work area to see if he needed anything. Lee Nelson was ready with a jack and wheel wrench to replace the right rear wheel spacer we had taken out prior to the feature. He observed that the car was too tight and needed to be loosened up. Lee replaced the spacer, bolted the wheel back on, and advised Jerry he was turning the fastest laps compared to everyone else on the track.

The race restarted and this time Jerry went to the bottom in turn three - and he drove right past Billy Engelhart, John Bankston, and Wayne Reutimann in turn four.

I blinked my eyes a couple times in order to believe what I had just witnessed, and made a mental note to try and remember to let that move sink in later.

Jerry got a little crossed-up on the cushion in turn four of the fifth lap, which allowed Bankston to catch up on the low side. They swapped lines going down the front straight and Jerry went to the bottom entering turn one to start the sixth lap. Bankston was less than two car lengths behind Jerry entering turn one. But Bankston slid to the top, lost some momentum, and Jerry put a 10 car length gap between the two of them going down the back straight.

On lap seven Jerry went around the outside of Woodward in turns one and two to pick up the second spot. Engelhart and Bankston split Woodward coming out of turn four and began a torrid battle for third place, with Engelhart on the top and Bankston on the bottom. They spent the majority of lap eight side by side running those same lines.

Entering turn one on lap nine Jerry came up on Lou Holland and slid up the track, and Bankston and Engelhart closed the gap quickly. Engelhart nearly got into Jerry's left rear coming out of turn two and had to take slight evasive action. This allowed Jerry to widen the gap a bit going down the back chute, but also let Bankston stay in the fight. Coming down the front chute Jerry and Engelhart split a lapped car, with Jerry on the bottom and Engelhart on top.

Jerry slide to the top in turn one of the 10th lap and took Engelhart's line away from him. This caused Engelhart to whoa it up big time in turn two, as his momentum nearly carried him into Jerry's rear bumper. If Engelhart didn't touch Jerry's bumper, it was the next closest thing to it. It's not every day you have someone who participated in the Indy 500 tapping on your rear bumper in a race at Knoxville. Meanwhile, as Jerry, Engelhart, and Bankston raged an entertaining yet nerve-wracking battle for second, race leader Mike Brooks had built a nearly straightaway lead.

But on this same lap the unthinkable happened.

Brooks entered the third corner and came fast upon a lapped car. John Allen, standing in his normal position in turn three, said he could see it coming from a mile away. Brooks ran over the wheel of the lapped car and took a vicious tumble into the turn three fence. He was uninjured, but the crash ended his night.

Jerry was now in the lead.

In the work area Jerry's first words were, "Who was it?"

Several people told him it was Brooks and that he was now the new leader. He was barraged with information about who was fast, what he should do on the restart, and what lines on the track he should run. Lee told him that he was wasting too much time sliding through the middle of the turns. I believe he was referring to the two times Jerry slid up the track in turn two, and was nearly run over by Englehart.

The race restarted and the second-running Engelhart got too high in turn three, and Bankston went under him to take that spot.

But Bankston wasn't done there.

He pulled along the inside of Jerry in turn four and they drag raced down the front straight.

Bankston stayed on the bottom and took the lead for a moment in turns one and two on the second attempt of the 10th lap. But Jerry had the momentum on top, fought like a dog, and regained the lead by the slimmest of margins going down the back chute – with Bankston right on his ass. Jerry kept to the cushion in three, Bankston stayed low, and drove right by on the inside of Jerry in turn four.

I cursed under my breath. It always seemed to happen this way, where eventually, almost inevitably, the race would be lost.

Jerry tucked in behind Bankston going down the front straight to start lap 11 and dove low into turn one, but Bankston already had that door shut. Jerry skated up to the cushion and lost all kinds of momentum, which allowed the third-running Englehart to close the gap. Englehart stayed within two and three car lengths for the rest of the lap.

They both entered turn one on the cushion on lap 12 and Englehart was back for a visit with Jerry's rear bumper, which seemed to have become his new best friend. But then Jerry settled down, stayed smooth on the cushion, and began to widen the gap between himself and Englehart going down the back straight.

Passing by the flag stand to start the 13th lap Jerry maintained a six or seven car length gap between himself and the third-running Englehart. Then Jerry set his sights on Bankston and went to work. He was patient, yet pursued Bankston aggressively.

At the start of the 14th lap he caught Bankston sliding up the track a bit. Jerry went around on the top and took the lead back in turn two, right in front of the suites of the National Sprint Car Hall of Fame & Museum. He started to stretch it out going down the back straight.

By the time he crossed the line to start lap 15 he had a several car length lead. Coming out of turn four he put a lapped car in between himself and Bankston and Englehart, who had now renewed their race amongst themselves.

The good news for us was that Bankston and Englehart got bottled up behind that lapped car in turns one and two of the 16th lap. The bad news for us was that Jerry got caught up behind two lapped cars of his own in front of the scoreboard in turns three and four. I thought for a moment that Jerry was going to try to split the lapped cars, which would not have ended well. Then I thought he was going to loop his car as he got on the binders, but he got it straightened out exiting turn four. Unfortunately all of this commotion allowed Bankston to come back to within striking distance again.

In turns one and two of the 17th lap Jerry got around the outside of a lapped car just in the nick of time, right before the lapper slid into the line Bankston was running. The lapped car acted as a downfield blocker for Jerry. He stretched his lead going down the back straight. Jerry stayed on the cushion and drove like a man possessed.

On lap 18 Jerry kept to the high side and drove by three more lapped cars. Could this be the night? But then the red flag flew again during the 19th lap for a wreck involving Farren. Another restart and another chance to lose this race.

Jerry once again received a bunch of advice in the work area. Several drivers, 410 drivers included, rushed over to share their knowledge. Sticking to my role as worrier I kept my mouth shut and quickly and quietly added a couple gallons of fuel to the tank. No way was he going to lose due to a lack of fuel.

The race restarted and immediately went yellow after one driver tried to make a pass before the restart cone on the backstretch. Unfortunately, Jerry showed his cards with the fast restart he had planned and executed. On the next restart the second-place Bankston would be ready. Bankston had been running well on the bottom of the track, but Jerry was well aware of that fact.

For this final restart and few laps I stood in turn four with my half jug of fuel and filthy clothes, and simply watched. Jerry had never been this close to winning a feature at Knoxville.

By this time in his sprint car racing career Jerry had won a couple of races at the Iowa State Fairgrounds. He was one of only a few drivers to beat Danny Young at that track when he took his first ever sprint car win.

I only have vague memories of that first win. I remember Danny being on Jerry's rear bumper throughout the race, and Jerry tagging the wall coming out of turn two at some point. I remember Danny giving Jerry a congratulatory embrace in the pits afterwards.

I remember Danny saying something to Jerry like, "We need to slow you down old man!"

I know I was happy, but I don't believe I appreciated it as much as I should have at the time.

Two weeks before this year's Masters – on the night Jerry threw the rod – he started on the pole at Knoxville and led the first six laps of a make-up feature before his dreams of winning went up in smoke, right along with his engine.

The previous week's features had been rained out, so the make-up was set for the first race that evening. It was definitely an odd and anxious feeling, knowing for the entire week that he would be starting on the pole.

The setup was perfect for him – starting on the pole on a narrow green racetrack with minimal chances of being passed. David Hesmer won that race and in the post-race interview even he said Jerry would have been hard to beat, had the engine not let go.

It just wasn't meant to be that night. Until now, that was the closest Jerry had ever come to winning at Knoxville.

On this final restart, Jerry went to the bottom of turn three and blocked Bankston's path. But he let his car drift up to the cushion in turn four, which allowed Bankston to move up on the inside. It also allowed Englehart, who stayed on the high side in turn three on the restart, to carry momentum and close the gap.

Jerry only had a two car length lead when he passed by the flag stand. For the majority of the race Jerry rode the high side on the cushion and Bankston preferred the low line. They weren't about to change things now, so that's how they entered

turn one. Bankston pulled even with Jerry in the middle of
turns one and two, but momentum allowed Jerry to pull out to
a six car length lead going down the back chute. He stayed on
the top and continued to stretch his lead.

I really wasn't sure he was going to do it until the white flag
was unfurled. He had a nice lead. By God, he was going to do
it.

As Jerry sped through three and four on that white flag lap,
I felt a quiet sense of relief. Jerry wasn't the only one who
wanted to win a race at Knoxville Raceway. It had been a
dream of mine to be a part of something like this since the very
first race I attended there.

In all my years of going to the races, the greatest sight I ever
saw was that red and white 12x first to pass under Norm
Wadle's double checkered flags. He did it. He won a feature at
Knoxville.

I stood there in stunned silence for a moment, and felt a
large grin spread across my face. I bent down, picked up the
half-empty fuel jug, and headed to the trailer.

Jerry was aglow when he climbed out of his sprint car back
at our pit stall. Several well-wishers were there to greet him,
and it seemed the whole pit area was happy to see Jerry finally
win one at Knoxville. It was probably the happiest I had ever
seen Jerry and he gave enthusiastic hugs to all around.

I took a seat on the left rear tire and just tried to soak it all
in and hold on to the moment. Jerry walked over grinning from
ear to ear, put an arm around my shoulders, and simply said,
"Thanks for your help, buddy."

I later learned that a few months prior, as Jerry's brother
Jim rested on his deathbed, that Jerry promised he would win a
race at Knoxville for him one day. Jerry's brother passed away
shortly thereafter, and Jerry had now fulfilled that promise. At
one point Jerry claimed to be an agnostic. If he was serious
when he made that claim, I think that all should have changed
after he won his only feature at Knoxville.

Jerry gave an interview in victory lane after the awards ceremony at the end of the night. It was recorded and can be seen on the Knoxville Raceway Weekly DVD available for purchase from the National Sprint Car Hall of Fame & Museum. The interview was conducted by veteran driver Tony Moro, who we raced against for a few years. I've done my best to transcribe the interview, and it went something like this:

Moro: "Jerry Crabb, this is probably one of the most pleasurable interviews I've ever had to do. Hey I tell you what, you had them covered. John Bankston made a run on you there, he passed you, did you ever think you could get him back?"

Jerry: "I didn't know, after he passed me, in the first half lap I said, damn, I'm going to have to settle for second again - and I wasn't likin' the thought. And then, I think he was running pretty much the middle, and down in three and four I tried down low, and it worked pretty good. I pulled up on him maybe fifty, seventy-five feet and I said, hey, there might be something here."

Moro: "You know, you're probably one of the most physically-fit people I know, and you're also over fifty. So that played maybe a little bit in consideration in outlasting some of the guys."

Jerry: "It could be, there's a few guys that fall out of the chair a little bit. But the guys that's finishing up front, Bankston's in good shape, obviously, you can tell by looking at him, and Englehart is too. Maybe a little farther back the guys are - they only do it once a year - and you can't do that. I mean you've got to be in the chair all the time, and you've got to get laps, and you've got to sweat, and you've got to feel the cramps."

Moro: "Jerry, the move that got you in position to win was on a restart."

Jerry: "I'm remembering this now, I'm thinking that there were two or three of them in a group that I went around at the time and probably surprised the heck out of Billy Englehart. I don't think he was expecting me that soon. I know he was worried about me a little bit maybe (grins). But I don't know, it seems like I got around three of them at one time and I was on my way, and probably disappointed them a little bit. But, you know, I've sat on that step down on the podium while he's been on the top before, so what goes around comes around I guess (laughs)."

Notes: Gary Wright won the accompanying All Star Circuit of Champions race, followed by Kenny Jacobs, Skip Jackson, Terry McCarl, and Joey Saldana. Heat races went to Nick Bellino, Jaymie Moyle, Sarah Fisher, and Don Droud, Jr. Leonard Lee won the B feature and Kenny Jacobs won the dash.

Postscript: Tragically, John Bankston lost his life in a sprint car accident at Eldora Speedway in August of 2001. God speed Mr. Bankston

1998 Masters Classic A Main
Knoxville Raceway, May 30, 1998

Finish	Driver, Hometown, Car# (Started)
1	Jerry Crabb, Des Moines, IA, 12x (10)
2	John Bankston, Beaumont, TX, 8 (4)
3	Billy Englehart, Oregon, WI, 10 (5)
4	Edd French, Keller, TX, 7777 (9)
5	Cliff Woodward, Kearney, MO, 1 (2)
6	Rick Ferkel, Tiffin, OH, 0 (14)
7	Bobby Allen, Hanover, PA, 48 (11)
8	Dave Heskin, Monticello, MN, 84 (6)
9	Lloyd Armey, Sedro Woolley, WA, 24c (7)
10	Chuck Graves, Chariton, IA, G2 (8)
11	Chris Maurer, Colfax, IA, 8B (13)
12	Harold McGilton, Fremont, OH, 81 (12)
13	Jerry Nemire, Erie, MI, 16 (18)
14	Lou Holland, McCallsburg, IA, 27 (16)
15	CJ Holley, Nelsonville, OH, 85 (15)
16	Shelby Steenson, Salina, KS, 6s (19)
17	Wayne Reutimann, Zephyr Hills, FL, 00 (1)
18	Dave Farren, Sr., Des Moines, IA, 48x (20)
19	Jon Backlund, Kansas City, MO, 21 (17)
20	Mike Brooks, Knoxville, IA, N14 (3)
21	Bill Smith, Worthington, MN, 33 (21)
22	Larry Hansen, Waverly, IA, 49 (22)
DNS	Earnest Jennings, Norman, OK, 61
DNS	Mike Thomas, Des Moines, IA, 37
DNS	Roy Jo Peltz, Maryville, MO, 90

Rookie of the Race: Bobby Allen

Source: knoxvilleraceway.com, track history section.

Career Masters Classic Finishes

Year	Started	Finished	Winner
1993	6th	2nd	Rick Ferkel
1994	18th	7th	Rick Ferkel
1995	18th	18th	Rick Ferkel
1996	18th	16th	Billy Engelhart
1997	8th	3rd	Billy Engelhart
1998	10th	1st	Jerry Crabb
1999	10th	5th	Roger Rager
2000	DNQ	DNQ	Terry Pletch
2001	20th	6th	Roger Rager
2002	6th	2nd	Mike Peters
2003	DNQ	DNQ	Jimmy Sills
2004	9th	7th	Jimmy Sills
2005	13th	6th	Roger Rager
2006 Masters	10th	8th	Shane Carson
2006 Young Guns vs. Masters	15th	13th	Johnny Anderson

Source: knoxvilleraceway.com, track history section.

"Well, I Like Racing Too"

Jerry experienced some struggles over the last few years racing sprint cars at Knoxville. When he first started racing there it was a disappointment to not finish in the top 10 of the feature. Then it was a disappointment to not make the feature. Toward the end of his career it was a happy occasion when he qualified for a feature. But as soon as you thought he would never qualify for another feature, he would go out and win a heat race, which only encouraged us, I think.

Towards the end of his career he experienced a series of accidents, the first of which gave him a concussion, and he experienced vertigo while racing. Typical old-school Jerry, he didn't tell any of us about this until he decided to hang it up for the year shortly after the Masters Classic.

Like everything, Knoxville changed over all those years. Engines in the 360 class went from something you could build in your garage for a few thousand dollars, to $30,000 plus powerplants that you never touched, purchased from a professional engine builder. Parts became lightweight and expensive. Not unlike most forms of racing, how fast you go depends on how much money you want to spend.

Jerry decided long ago that he would not spend that kind of money to stay in this sport, which automatically made it very difficult to remain competitive. And sponsors don't give money to very many drivers who are in their sixties.

Over the final few years Jerry also ran both a winged and non-winged 305 cubic inch sprint car at various tracks in Iowa, and experienced considerable success.

In 2004 he placed second in the winged and fourth in the non-winged features on the same night for a special 305 race they held at Knoxville. That was one of my most enjoyable nights helping Jerry since we had to remove or replace the wings, as well as make other adjustments, every time he came off the track.

At the end of the 2004 and beginning of the 2005 seasons he won three 305 features at the Bloomfield, Iowa, track.

That class reminds me of what the 360 class used to be - low budget guys who want to find a way to have fun and keep racing, or drivers looking for a way to gain experience to move up to a higher class. However, inevitably teams in that class are spending more money to gain speed, just like in every other form or class of racing.

And now it was coming to an end. Or so I thought.

On the Friday night two weeks after my 2006 annual call to Jerry, I returned home late from a client's golf tournament in Omaha and listened to a voice message.

It said, "Toddly, this is Jerry. I'm thinking about taking the car to Knoxville tomorrow if you're interested. Call me."

I kind of took this with a grain of salt. Yes, I like racing. But the last few years as I helped Jerry as we struggled with his race car, I began questioning whether it was all worth it. I kind of enjoyed being home on the Saturday nights he didn't race. Call it burnout, or whatever.

The next day at Knoxville, after unloading the car and equipment, I asked Jerry, almost incredulously, "What are you doing? Are you just shaking the car down for Masters or what?"

"I don't know," he said, "I'll have to see how I feel." He then added, "You know, I really enjoyed not racing."

To which I replied, again somewhat incredulously, "So what are you doing here?"

He simply replied with a laugh, "Well, I like racing too."

And that says it all.

I think everyone understands when drivers say, "I'll quit when I know I'm not competitive," and I completely respect those decisions.

But people have trouble understanding when drivers continue to race when they may not be as competitive as they once were. Well, it's really pretty easy to understand. They just like to race. I respect that decision too.

So we raced, if that's what you want to call it, through the weeks leading up to The Masters. Mostly we fought a fuel problem that simply would not allow the car to take off the way it should.

He did manage to earn a fifth-place finish in a heat race one night, only to be disqualified for running illegal tires. Knoxville had changed a rule after the start of the season from requiring a certain compound hardness of rear tires, to requiring a specific set of rear tires - which Jerry didn't own and wasn't about to purchase.

Once in the tech area following the heat race, where the top five finishers were required to report immediately after the race, track officials discovered Jerry's illegal tires. They were the proper hardness, just not the correct set of tires.

The top official at the track was summoned to the tech area, and simply stated, "Your tires are illegal Jerry."

"They're all I've got," Jerry replied.

"All right, get it out of here," the official responded.

So rather than possibly starting at the tail of the A feature, or maybe the front of the B, Jerry had to start at the tail of the B that night. Jerry took it in stride though. He knew his tires weren't right - he was just trying to get the car ready for The Masters.

The next week Dave Cornwell, the long-time 4-wheeler operator, stopped by our pit stall. He said to me, "Hey, what would Jerry do without you?"

"Probably just keep racing," I said.

"Which tire was illegal last week?" he asked.

"Both," I replied.

He just shook his head and chuckled as he drove off.

That same night Jerry signed up for The Masters, which he nearly forgot to do, since the race was scheduled for the next

Friday night. In the ticket office where he paid the entry fee he took a little grief for being disqualified the week prior, in the vein of, "What do you think you were trying to pull?"

Jerry just told them, "Those tires are five years old."

Typical old-school Jerry.

The Masters came and went that year without much notice to the racing world. Less than twenty 50+ year-olds signed up for the event (the inaugural race in 1993 had 42 entrants, where Jerry placed second to Rick Ferkel).

For the 2006 running they tried something different. They invited the top 25 in points from the Knoxville 360 class and called it "Young Guns vs. Masters."

A challenge race was held between the two groups after the 50-year-old and over drivers raced in The Masters feature for $1000 to win, and the Young Guns participated in one of their own. Then they took the top 10 from each of those races and threw them together for a $1000 to win challenge race. Personally I thought this sounded like a recipe for disaster, but thankfully I was wrong.

Jerry's car was popping and banging like a popcorn maker due to the ongoing fuel problem. We thought we had it figured out after he pulled into the pits following his time trial and discovered the car's left header was blown out near one of the exhaust ports.

But after replacing the headers with some borrowed from Johnny Anderson, one of the regulars there to race with the Young Guns, the car continued to pop and bang and just refused to run right. He still managed to finish 8th in The Masters race and 13th in the challenge race. Shane Carson won The Masters, and Johnny Anderson won both the Young Guns and challenge races.

At some point during the night I walked by myself in the middle of the infield between the trucks and trailers, carrying two empty fuel jugs on my way to the fuel truck. I looked around, listened to the cars on the track, and caught a whiff of diesel fuel from the tow vehicles. I smiled to myself and thought, "Man, I still love this stuff."

After the races as Jerry, Jan, Tracie, and I loaded the car and equipment, Jim Harris walked by with a smile on his face and asked me, "You're still doing this?"

"I guess so," I replied, motioning to Jerry, "as long as he keeps doing this."

The next week Jerry knew he wouldn't race because he was attending his grandson's birthday party. The following Saturday I received a call from him saying he wasn't going to race that night, and wasn't sure about the rest of the season. This was the day after a Minnesota man lost his life in an accident at the "Nostalgia at Knoxville" show, where they held an exhibition race with restored race cars from yesteryear.

I heard from him again later that summer, right before the Nationals, when he called to see if I wanted a pit pass for the event. Like usual I had those days off from work, but I turned the pass down and spent the time laying patio blocks outside my basement door. That was the first year I hadn't attended a single night of the Nationals since 1985.

I haven't heard from Jerry since.

One way or another the day will come when Jerry will stop racing, and it may have already happened and I don't know it. I'm not sure if he knows. Maybe he will at least continue to race in The Masters, maybe he won't.

If he is done, I'll miss seeing Jerry every week during the summer. He is a true character and they just don't make them like him anymore. I'll miss him grabbing me by the arm and leading me around the car, pointing out the changes he made in the past week. Or his mischievous grin when he says, "Hey, I haven't touched the car since last year." I'll miss the camaraderie. I can only hope that some of his "old school" rubbed off on me over all those years.

In any case, my small part in this crazy little world of sprint car racing allowed me to meet some great people and collect memories that will last a lifetime. I think I'm just now beginning to realize how lucky I was to be a part of something I simply loved to do. If I never go to Knoxville again, I'll always cherish those memories.

But if Jerry gives me the call and says he's taking that 12x to Knoxville again, you can bet I'll be there. Because, like Jerry said, even though I liked not racing, well, I like racing too.

Epilogue

It's been over 11 years since Jerry's last race at Knoxville, which is also around the same time I first sat down to write a version of the preceding pages. A lot can happen in a person's life in that amount of time. In my case an unexpected divorce, and the passing of my father. Kids growing up, going to college and leaving the state for work, and helping them deal with their own life trials and tribulations. And experiencing a true empty nest.

I saw Jerry and Jan, and John, a few years ago at the visitation for Ron Nelson, who had succumbed to a fight with cancer. I wish I had kept in contact with Ron, as he was one of a kind and I'm glad I knew him.

I was happy to hear that Jerry got a chance to visit Ron in the hospital prior to his passing, and I wish I could have been a fly on the wall for that conversation. At the visitation I was able to see some of Ron's racing memorabilia, including a photo of all of us on the front stretch at the fairgrounds from Jerry's very first sprint car feature win. Jerry, Jan, and John hadn't seemed to have changed a bit.

I did a Google Maps search on Jerry's old shop the other day, just to see if she was still standing. It was disheartening to see that she was not, and had been replaced by a pristine new building.

However when I drilled down to the street level I was comforted to see the familiar old gal staring back at me. She looked a little worse for the wear, suffering from years of neglect and abandonment, and wore "FOR SALE MAKE OFFER" signage. I quickly took screen shots from different angles, as if the image would disappear at any moment. I spent many hours and made many memories in that old building over the years, but time marches on.

And thanks to social media, I saw Jerry had raced in a few 3-wheeler indoor races in the last couple of years. In his 70's. Racing truly is hard to get out of your blood.

I have been back to Knoxville, and it's a little strange going there, not really having a reason to be there. My cousin and I have attended a couple of nights of the Nationals the past few years – even paying the $50 for a pit pass that I said I'd never do. It gives me the chance to have my once-a-year visit with Ted Hulgan, who still drives a push truck at the track every week.

I've also went a few times to weekly shows and sat in the top row of the grandstand and caught up with old friends - the brothers Mike and Jim Harris - who still attend every week.

Jim does some work for sprintsource.com and the national 410 rookie of the year poll. Mike recently emailed me lists of nationwide all-time feature winners and track champions. They both still know more about sprint car racing than I ever will.

Mike had to deal with some medical issues recently but only missed a few weeks of racing. Someone asked his wife when the last time was that he missed two weeks in a row at Knoxville. She told them never, unless it was due to rain outs.

In 2016 I stumbled upon dirtvision.com, the website that allows a person to sign up for pay-per-view live World of Outlaws sprint car races. More importantly it allows you to watch all races they video for free, in the on-demand section, a week or so after the race.

I have taken full advantage of this, watching every race they videoed in 2016 and 2017, along with all in their Classics section, plus many of the previous years' races. I've also fully utilized their free audio broadcasts of every World of Outlaws race, and have spent many a night in the man cave playing pool while listening to races from all over the country. The site has renewed my interest.

My cousin and I also traveled to the Spencer, Iowa, Clay County Fair World of Outlaws race in September of 2016. We spent a couple of days in the Iowa Great Lakes area fishing, in addition to attending the race. We went again in 2017 for an Interstate Racing Association (IRA) sanctioned race. It might be turning into an annual trip.

I bought Bob Trostle's autobiography, *Life's Tough on the Circuit*, edited by Larry Weeks. There is so much information in that book that I've read through it five times so far. I think I'll just keep re-reading it. I read a couple of pages every day before work, and it's a good way to start the day. Hard to believe Bob Trostle is gone.

I decided to write this right after Jerry retired as a way to keep memories from fading, and also for my kids if they ever came across it, so they would know what their dad was doing during all those Saturday nights I was away at Knoxville.

I realize my recollections are not exceptional, just mine. They are a drop in the bucket of the thousands of stories that could be told by people involved in racing.

Professional race teams are well-known and their stories are documented regularly and thoroughly, and rightly so. But keep in mind there are hundreds of race teams at dozens of dirt tracks who race all across the country every year, for nothing more than the love of the race.

I haven't been able to determine if sprint car racing attracts interesting characters, or if being one is a requirement to participate, but the sport seems to be chock-full of them. I'm willing to bet you could go to any dirt track and talk to the last place finisher in the lowest consolation race, and they would have great stories to tell. I like hearing those too.

God Speed

On Saturday, January 6, 2018, I spent a quiet afternoon proofreading the preceding pages, making changes that never seemed to come to an end. I checked my phone and was surprised to see I had missed a call from John. Rather than listen to the message he left I simply returned his call.

My heart sank when he told me Jerry had passed away that afternoon. The news took the wind out of my sails and shook me to my core. I thought the man was indestructible. It was three years to the day since I gave the eulogy at my father's funeral.

I got on Facebook and confirmed the news, and read several tributes to Jerry. I received a friend request from Shane, and shortly thereafter was tagged in a tribute of his own. I sent a friend request to Jan.

I read the heartbreaking posts from his grandchildren. Jerry adored his grandchildren, and they adored him. One post documented Jerry's medical procedures over the years. The list included the previously noted knee replacement after the 1999 360 Knoxville Nationals. Both shoulders and both hips replaced. Wrist and hernia surgeries. The broken ribs, collapsed lung, and cuts he received from the time he somehow ran himself over with his tractor while working at his farm.

In the following days and a follow up call with John, he relayed that he believed our old friend Brad Watson had passed away in recent months. I got on the internet and confirmed. He died of a heart attack the previous September. Fifty-six years old.

Through the magic of social media I tracked down Smooth and gave him the news. Besides the circumstances, it was nice to catch up. He wasn't going to be able to attend the Celebration of Life due to prior commitments. I know Jerry would understand.

As word spread I received a text from Jimmy Freel, an old grade school/little league baseball teammate/high school/band dad/racing buddy. He told me about an interaction he had with Jerry that I hadn't heard before.

It seems Jimmy was racing a 4-wheeler at the Winter Dome around thirty years ago, when he tagged the wall and dumped his ride. As he sat on the track and attempted to gather himself, Jerry and another fellow came over to check on Jimmy.

Jimmy took his helmet off. Jerry told him, "NEVER take your helmet off after a wreck. You don't want the people to see the face of the fool who just wrecked in front of them. Wait until you get back to the trailer."

Then Jimmy put his helmet back on.

Then Jerry and the other fellow had a good laugh.

Yup. That sounds like Jerry Crabb.

I attended Jerry's Celebration of Life held at the American Legion Hall in Indianola the following Wednesday. His handcrafted 3-wheeler sat in a trailer parked outside the front entrance. It had been many years since I laid eyes on the beast in person. Back in the day he dominated races riding that thing. The work of art belongs in a museum somewhere.

I walked through the doors and by chance got in the receiving line right behind Mike Harris. We each gave Jan a hug and offered our condolences. Then Jan told us the story.

It seems on that fateful Saturday morning, Jerry was up early. At 74 years old he was preparing to make the trip to Mason City to race his 3-wheeler in an indoor Coke syrup race. That sticky substance is used as a way to add traction on hard surfaces for many of these types of indoor races. He wanted to go there to practice so he didn't "look like a fool" at the Battle at the Barn races held in the Jacobsen Building on the Iowa State Fairgrounds later in the month. But he collapsed on the living room floor due to a bleed in his brain. How appropriate that his final day consisted of preparations to compete in a race.

Jerry was life-flighted to a hospital in Des Moines and Jan had to make the trip there by herself by car, driving from their southern Iowa farm. By the time she arrived they already had Jerry on a ventilator. He passed at 1:12 p.m. He just had to get one more "1" with his signature "12."

Many family members were able to say their good-byes, and Jan believes Jerry heard them. I believe so too.

Unexplainable things happen when a person transitions from this life to the hereafter. Well, actually I believe they are very explainable.

On my dad's final day he never woke up as he rested in a hospice bed. He was placed there only three days earlier after his doctors inevitably surrendered in their battle of balance between his heart and kidney failure. My mom wouldn't leave his side.

Throughout the day hospice staff gave estimates of time he had left, which shrank from days, to hours, to before the next day break. Mom only wished she could tell him she loved him one more time. Hospice staff ensured us he could hear our words.

Later that night after staff repositioned him in his bed, Dad opened his eyes for a moment and attempted to lift his head. We all rushed to the bedside and told him we loved him, and he uttered an "I love you too." And then he drifted off again. Mom's wish had been granted.

Just before midnight Mom said she just had to use the restroom. She still had not left my dad's side. She wanted someone to have hands laid on Dad at all times, so I took her place at the head of the bed. I placed my right hand on his right shoulder and my left hand on his head, as he laid on his left side. My daughter held his hand on the other side of his bed, and my son stood behind her.

My mom left the room and couldn't have made it to the restroom before my dad took his final breath. I told him it was

175

okay, he didn't have to fight anymore. He had waited until Mom left the room. One more act of protection.

My sister and brother-in-law, niece, and my kids and I were with him as he slipped away as peacefully as you could possibly imagine. I kissed his forehead, and then pressed the call-nurse button.

We waited in the room with Dad until the person from the funeral home arrived. Mom asked if I would say a few words at Dad's funeral in the coming days. That's not something you can say no to. Strangely, I had already thought through what I would say three months earlier after Dad had an episode in a hospital emergency room and CPR had brought him back. I wasn't planning or expecting to give a eulogy, but something drew me to prepare for it.

The person from the funeral home arrived and we went to the hospice chapel, where they light a candle for the recently deceased. We each wrote a message in the book they keep in the room.

We walked out of the building and saw them loading Dad in the hearse. We each got in our own cars and Mom got in mine, and we left her car there to deal with later. I pulled onto Merle Hay Road in Johnston and went south, and stopped in the left turn lane at the stoplight to head east onto I-80.

But the dang light turned green for traffic to go straight through the intersection and had skipped over my signal to turn left. It was in the 3:00 a.m. hour and there was no traffic. I looked in the rearview mirror and saw headlights approaching and recognized it was my sister's car. I looked in the left sideview mirror and saw another set of headlights approaching in the other left turn lane.

The vehicle pulled alongside and I looked over at it, and said, "There's Dad." It was the hearse. Then the left turn signal turned green. We followed the hearse until the turnoff at the bypass to make our way to Runnells. We were given one more trip as a family.

The point of all this is that unexplainable yet very explainable things happen when a person transitions away from this life. That's why I know Jerry heard their goodbyes. I also believe he heard the ones from all of us who weren't in that room.

A steady stream of family, friends, and race folks made their way in and out throughout Jerry's three hour Celebration of Life. At one point there was nowhere to sit. I believe the crowd would have been even larger had the Chili Bowl Midget Nationals in Tulsa not been taking place that week, as many area race people take in that event annually. Jerry would be the first to understand an absence due to attending a race.

I caught up with Mike, Shane, Tracie, and John and his wife. I saw Detrick from across the room but we didn't get a chance to speak. I said a few words to Jeff Morris as he was on his way out. He's still working on sprint cars.

I listened in on a conversation between John and Mackie Heimbaugh. In 1983 Mackie became Knoxville Raceway's very first Limited (360) points champion. He knows what he is talking about. Mackie looks like he could still strap into a sprint car and go racing tomorrow.

John and Mackie talked about Jerry and how he was nearly unbeatable racing his handcrafted 3-wheeler. Mackie said he respected Jerry's sprint car career, his longevity, and how he spent his life doing what he loved. He described how Jerry was a sprint car driver who could turn in a great performance on any given Saturday night. That's a damn good assessment.

I spoke with Jerry's son Robin, who is an attorney in the Washington, D.C., area. I had met him once, maybe twice, many years ago. I told him how much I'll miss his dad and that I had learned a lot from Jerry over the years. He asked me what was the most important thing I learned from his dad over the time I spent on his pit crew. That's a difficult question for me to nail down. I told him I respected how Jerry lived life to the fullest and on his own terms. How he was not intimidated by anything. How he unknowingly taught me to never be afraid to take a chance and try new things. I loved his old-school persona. That answer is true but really doesn't do the question justice. I can imagine that it was not always easy to be the son of Jerry Crabb.

Many of Jerry's trophies from years gone by — but not nearly all of them - sat on the tables for visitors to view while they ate their meals. I had to chuckle when I saw the bowls of popcorn, peanut M&M's, and box of toothpicks on the buffet line. Those were always staples in the Crabb pit area. The pulled-pork and sides were delicious, but I just couldn't clean my plate.

Other tables were set up with Jerry's photos, awards, and mementoes from high school and days of military service. His helmet was on display and I picked it up and held it one more time. I held it many times over the years as I waited for him to strap into his sprint car. There were three tear-offs left on the shield, patiently waiting for the next race.

I saw that damn picture of me wearing that damn sports bra. I thought, "Here's my chance to rid the earth of that thing!" But Tracie mentioned she had a copy in safe keeping, so destroying it would have done me no good.

Jerry was cremated and his urn sat on one of the tables. He was also an organ donor, and John and I couldn't help but wonder and joke about just what exactly would have been suitable to donate, given Jerry's medical history. We could envision him salvaging some of his replacement parts and fashioning them into something to make his 3-wheeler go faster. Jerry would have appreciated the humor.

There was a lot of laughter and storytelling about Jerry. It was a good night and I think he approved.

At one point I overheard Jan tell someone that on a recent morning, as she was preparing for the day, she looked to the sky, pointed her finger, and sternly said, "I know you're up there Crabb – you were wrong – I know you're up there!"

I believe she's right. At one point Jerry told me he was an agnostic. That didn't mean he didn't believe, he just needed proof. He now has that proof. I can imagine Jerry and Nelson up there in heaven, and Jerry giving Nelson grief about not doing something right.

Before leaving I finally worked up the courage to tell Jan about my little project here. I told her that even though I hadn't kept in contact after Jerry retired from racing, I still thought of them often and considered them as family. She replied that if we had all gotten together again, it would have been just like it was back in those good old days. I believe that's true. I obtained her email address and told her I would send a copy of the work-in-process. I guess I'm committed now.

I first started working on this right after Jerry retired from sprint car racing in 2006. At that point it was a pretty rough version. At the time I really didn't know what it was, if anything, and I guess I still don't know. I emailed Tom Schmeh at the National Sprint Car Hall of Fame & Museum and asked if he would care to take a look. He said he would be happy to give it a read.

I didn't know Tom, although in the past I had chatted with him a few times when I visited the Hall of Fame. He was always kind and eager to talk sprint car racing. We had discussed how we both made our first visits to Knoxville Raceway in 1985, and both witnessed Doug Wolfgang win the Nationals that year.

I emailed that version to Tom and halfway expected I'd never hear from him again. But I received an email from him a couple of weeks later. He said he enjoyed the manuscript, but wasn't sure if there was anything I could do with it. He knew of others who had attempted to publish books and the difficulties they faced. I presumed he was being kind and let the file sit on my old Windows XP desktop.

It sat there until I stumbled upon it again in the summer of 2017. I wonder if I really stumbled upon it, or if something drew me back. My interest in racing had renewed.

I played around with it that summer, and began to question the purpose. Was it just for fun? Was it my midlife crisis? Others buy a Harley for their midlife crisis, I attempt to write a book about sprint car racing.

I contemplated showing it to Jerry, but was very hesitant. I hadn't kept in contact with him since he retired, and he had no clue of my little project. I wasn't sure how he would take it. And I just didn't have it to the point where I was ready to share.

I worked up the courage to tell my cousin about it on the four hour trip to the Iowa Great Lakes in September. We were on our way to do some fishing and take in the sprint car race at the 2017 Clay County Fair.

He was encouraging and said he would be glad to read the manuscript and offer advice. I told him I definitely wanted his honest opinion, especially if he thought my writing was stupid.

179

I also told him if he thought it was the dumbest thing he ever read but didn't have the heart to tell me, since he's my cousin, that I would get the gist if I never heard a word from him about it again.

I sent it to him the Monday after we returned - and didn't hear from him for two weeks. By then I presumed he thought it was terrible and took the route of not mentioning anything. But on the way back from a trip to view the Sammy Swindell exhibit at the Hall of Fame he told me he had reviewed it, thought it was a worthwhile endeavor, and was making notes of his suggestions.

It was originally written for our little group, and I thought I would print a few copies for Jerry and his family and a few for my own. I could throw it out on Amazon in case anyone else wanted a copy. But my cousin suggested I broaden the potential audience to include the casual race fan and those unfamiliar with the sport. He enjoyed the semi-technical aspects and thought I should add more of that type of text. I worked on it further and the "A Night at the Races" chapter doubled in size. I told him if I went in further detail, at some point I'd be describing how I tied my shoes.

I continued working on it and was almost ready to show Jerry at the time of his passing. I wish I hadn't waited. I believe he would have gotten a kick out of it.

I decided to go ahead and publish it unaltered, after receiving Jan's okay. It's self-published through the website createspace.com, which includes a feature to determine the amount of royalty the author will receive. My original thought was to set the royalty to zero, because whatever this is it was never meant to be about trying to make money. The cost would have been whatever the website charged to manufacture and publish, which I'm sure includes a built in profit, since they are a business.

But when I got to that point I found you can't actually set the royalty - it's automatically calculated. Even if you set the price to the lowest amount the website allows, it still calculates some sort of royalty, much to my chagrin.

So there will be some sort of royalty involved. I don't know the amount or if it will change at some point. But rest assured that whatever that royalty turns out to be, for the time being, it's going to Jan.

God speed Jerry. We sure had a lot of fun. I'll see you again one day.

Postscript: They honored Jerry during pre-race ceremonies at the "Battle at the Barn" Coke syrup races on Saturday, January 20, 2018. The Midwest Trike Outlaws racing organization announced that they retired Jerry's #12.

I cannot think of a more appropriate tribute.

Jerry's handcrafted 3-wheeler in the infield at the "Battle at the Barn" January 20, 2018. (Battle at the Barn photo)

Competitors in Heat Races, Consolation Features, and A Features at Knoxville Raceway from 1990 to 2006

While completing research in the track history section on knoxvilleraceway.com, I came across the results of Jerry's very first heat race in 1990. This was when he drove a 410 cubic inch sprint car for a car owner, prior to teaming up with John on their own 360. His first heat race at Knoxville took place during the spring World of Outlaws show that year and was won by Jeff Swindell, followed by Stevie Smith and Steve Kinser. Other drivers in that heat included Kevin Doty, Mike Brooks, Jerry Janssen, Jeff Tuttle, Jaymie Moyle, Tom Whiting, Bob White, and Randy Smith.

It made me wonder about all the drivers Jerry raced with at Knoxville throughout his career. So I went on a mission and searched for his name in the results for each year from 1990 to 2006. I copied and pasted the names of all drivers he competed with in heat races, dashes, consolation features, and A features. I left out the races where he did not start, and the names of those who did not start in his races.

There are 534 names on the list. It's an impressive list.

It proves that if you race at Knoxville long enough, you eventually race against everybody. The following pages contain that list.

Competitors in Heat Races, Consolation Features, and A Features at Knoxville Raceway from 1990 to 2006

Source: knoxvilleraceway.com, track history section

Craig Agan
Jon Agan
James Alexander
Mitchell Alexander
Stacey Alexander
Terry Alexander
Jim Alexander Jr.
Bobby Allen
Billy Alley
Chuck Amati
Mark Amenda
Paul Andersen
Billy Anderson
Bob Anderson
Dave Anderson
Don Anderson
Johnny Anderson
Kip Anderson
Nate Anderson
Randy Anderson
Ryan Anderson
Bart Andrews
Brent Antill
Lloyd Armey
George Austin III
Jon Backlund
Tim Baker
Gregg Bakker

Larry Ball Jr.
Steve Ballenger
John Bankston
Allen Barr
Rodney Baughman
B.J. Baze
Joe Beaver
Dave Becker
Bobby Becker Jr.
Lloyd Beckman
Billy Bell
Robert Bell
Nick Bellino
James Bevan
Will Bevan
Beau Binder
Tod Bishop
John Blurton
Duane Bonini Jr.
Clay Bontrager
Patrick Bourke
Joe Boyles
Seth Brahmer
Virgil Brandt
Rick Branham
Pete Braswell
Steve Breazeale
Ken Brewer

Mike Brooks

Brian Brown

David Brown

Dean Brown

Frank Brown

Stew Brown

Toby Brown

Fran Bruns

Boyd Burnham

Pete Butler

Scott Cahill

Bill Campbell

Shane Carson

Bryan Castine

Rich Cerveny

Mike Chadd

Ken Chapman

Toby Chapman

Daniel Coggeshell

Randy Combs

Rex Combs

Ryan Coniam

Don Cooper

Joe Cooper

Jon Corbin

Greg Coverdale

Chris Coyle

Pete Crall

Travis Cram

Mike Crawford

Tim Crawley

Jim Cress

Gerald Cressman

John Cressman

Erin Crocker (Evernham)

Jim Cruise

Paul Crusan

Greg Curzon

J D Johnson

Ronnie Daniels

Jason Danley

Todd Daun

Jimmy Davies

Tom Davies

Kurt Davis

Don Dawson II

Don Dawson Sr.

Gary Dean

Steve Dean

Tim Deaver

Bruce Defries

Harry Delamont

Kevin Delong

Shawn Deman

Mark Detrick

Larry Dickson

Bruce Divis

Craig Dollansky

Tim Doogs

Doran Doty

Kevin Doty

Mike Dreiling

Randy Droescher

Bruce Drottz

Don Droud Jr.

Max Dumesny

Billy Dusenbery	Jesse Giannetto
Mark Dyer	Alan Gilbertson
Nick Eastin	Johnny Gilbertson
Andy Eatwell	Howie Gleason
Rob Edwards	Kevin Gobrecht
Jon Eldreth	Donny Goeden
Michael Elmore	Brett Golik
Mike Elmore	Chuck Graves
Dave Engebretson	Terry Gray
Billy Engelhart	John Greenwood
Rick England	Miles Grein
Archie Ergenbright	Jeff Griffis
Ed Ergenbright	Bryan Grimes
Walt Esch	French Grimes
Nate Estal	Scott Grissom
Tommie Estes Jr.	Greg Gunderson
RC Faigle	Chuck Gurney
Dave Farren Sr.	Jody Hahn
Rick Ferkel	Jeff Haines
Jamie Ferrell	Brandon Hainline
Roger Fickett	Dave Hall
Matt Folstad	John Hall
Jeff Fort	John Haluska
Rod Foster	Kenny Hansen
Daniel Frederick	Larry Hansen
Edd French	Butch Hanssen
Karl Freyer	Matt Harms
Todd Frisbie	Darl Harrison
Ned Fry	Jac Haudenschild
Joe Gaerte	Bobby Hawks
Clint Garner	Nick Haygood
Jim Gates	Frankie Heimbaugh
Steve Gennetten	Mackie Heimbaugh

John Helm
Greg Helms
Rod Henderson
Dave Hendricks
Wally Henson
Mike Heronemus
Johnny Herrera
Dave Heskin
Davey Heskin
DJ Heskin
David Hesmer
Brian Hetrick
Josh Higday
Keith Hightshoe
Bill Hildreth
Bob Hildreth
Andy Hillenburg
Terry Hinck
Dion Hindi
Chuck Hines
Fran Hogue
Dave Hollamon
Lou Holland
CJ Holley
Tim Holzworth
Hooker Hood
Mike Houseman
Mike Houseman Jr.
Dale Howard
Jan Howard
Aaron Hubler
Jay Hughes
Brandon Hull

Kevin Huntley
Danny Hutchins
Rick Ideus
Robert Jackson
Skip Jackson
Ryan Jamison
Jerry Janssen
Danny Jennings
Earnest Jennings
Lonnie Jensen
Roy Jo Peltz
Eric Jobe
Bob Johnson
Steve Johnson
Wayne Johnson
Jeff Johnson (Ames)
Jeff Johnson (Indianola)
Jimmy Johnston
Don Jones
Greg Jones
Jeff Jones
Marlon Jones
Michael Jones
Randy Jones
Keith Kauffman
John Kearney
Bill Keester
Tim Kelly
Kim Kennedy
Darrin Key
Bob Kinser
Steve Kinser
Regan Kitchen

Jay Klabunde
Mike Kostic
Joe Kouba
Jeff Krutsinger
Rob Kubli
Bob Lamb
John Lambertz
Greg Lanc
Craig Lane
Ronald Laney
Ken Lange
Loren Langerud
David Langford
Doug Larsen
Danny Lasoski
Randy Laube
Mike Lauterborn
Toby Lawless
Eddie Leavitt Jr.
Terry Ledger
Leonard Lee
Donald Lee Friesz
Ray Lee Goodwin
Randy Lee Jones
Garry Lee Maier
Tommy Lee Williams
Dwain Leiber
Tom Lenz
Greg Leonard
Drew Lewis
Shane Liebig
Dustin Lindquist
Bill Livezey

Ricky Logan
Hank Lower
Jeff Lowery
Toni Lutar
Lewis Lynch
Bronson Maeschen
Dick Mahoney
Chris Mallicoat
David Marshall
Jake Martens
Galen Martin
Randy Martin
Chris Martinez
Adam Mason
Eric Mason
Mike Masonbrink
Brett Mather
Chris Maurer
Bob Mays
Terry McCarl
Tony McCarthy
Dale McCarty
Rick McClure
Bill McCroskey
Jim McElreath
Chuck McGillivray
Harold McGilton
Bill Mellenberndt
Ryan Menninga
Billy Mentgen
Troy Meyer
Curt Michael
Sean Michael

Competitors in Heat Races, Consolation Features, and A Features at
Knoxville Raceway from 1990 to 2006 (Cont)

Dave Middleswart
Tom Mikels
Tommy Mikels
Joe Miller
Midge Miller
Randi Miller
Bobby Mincer
Jeff Mitrisin
Kim Mock
Wayne Modjeski
Mitchell Moore
Pat Moore
Dennis Moore Jr.
Sean Moran
Chris Morgan
Matt Moro
Tony Moro
Steve Morris
Nate Mosher
Gary Moyer
Jaymie Moyle
Al Murie
John Naida
Richard Nash
Dave Nederhoff
Larry Neighbors
Scott Neitzel
John Nelson
Lee Nelson
Jerry Nemire
Tim Newman
Jim Nichols
Tracy Nichols

Tony Norem
Colin Northway
Billy Ray Olson
Dan Oswalt
Jason Pardock
Justin Parrish
Christi Passmore
Glen Passmore
Glen Passmore Jr.
Jamie Passmore
Jim Payne
Brad Peltz
Jace Pennetta
Wayne Pennington
Ed Perryman
Jake Peters
Mike Peters
Steve Pfaff
Rager Philips
Steve Pickering
Larry Pinegar II
Brad Pinkerton
Daryn Pittman
Terry Pletch
Jerry Potter
Rusty Potter
Ned Powers
Russ Prather
George Prosser
Mike Przyborski
David Pyatt
Chad Radel
Roger Rager

Benny Rapp

Ken Ratchford

Keith Rauch

Stacy Redmond

Wayne Redmond

Mike Reinke

Wayne Reutimann

Trevor Reynolds

Todd Ribick

Rod Richards

Steve Richards

Jerry Richert Jr.

Frank Riddle

Travis Rilat

Joe Roach

Dr. Robert Altmeyer

Bill Robertson

Scott Robertson

Gerry Robison

Manny Rockhold

Greg Roorda

Ed Rotert

Kelly Rowe

Joe Rynearson

Rick Salem

Natalie Sather

Micah Schliemann

Brian Schnee

Bart Schneiderman

Josh Schneiderman

Eric Schrock

John Schulz

Tommy Scott

Dustin Selvage

John Sernett

Kent Severson

Tim Shaffer

Brian Shearer

Roger Short

Jason Sides

Jimmy Sills

Bill Smith

Chadd Smith

Jarod Smith

Oscar Smith

Randy Smith

Rick Smith

Stevie Smith

Tod Smith

Smokey Snellbaker

Dwight Snodgrass

Rick Sorem

Dick Spadaro

Todd Splain

Tim St. Arnold

Ray Staats

Red Stauffer

Daryl Steenhoek

Shelby Steenson

Matt Stephenson

Donnie Steward

Tony Stewart

Tom Stookey

Brad Strayer

Jim Strobel

Bill Stroud

Competitors in Heat Races, Consolation Features, and A Features at
Knoxville Raceway from 1990 to 2006 (Cont)

Steve Suever

Craig Sunt

Mark Swanson

Jeff Swindell

Sammy Swindell

Lyle Sylvester

Jeff Tanksley

Kevin Tanner

Brooke Tatnell

Bob Thoman

Al Thomas

Mike Thomas

Terry Thomas

Bob Thompson

Tyler Thompson

Dan Thornburg

Curtis Thorson

Terry Thorson

Chris Tice

John Tierney

Mark Toews

Jay Totten

Ken Townsand

Mike Trent

Rodney Turner

Jeff Tuttle

Mike Twedt

Bill Utz

Leroy Van Connett

Dave Van Heukelom

Duane Van Heukelom

John VanDenBerg

Eric VanderPloeg

Nate VanHaaften

Billy Vielhauer

Ryan Voss

Mike Waddell

Randy Wagler

Earl Wagner

Alan Walker

Tyler Walker

Chris Walraven

Stevie Walsh

Steve Wares

Steve Wasson

AJ Weaver

Larry Webb

Larry Weeks

Rick Weld

Taylor Weld

Todd Wessels

Dave Westercamp

Bob Weuve

Bob White

Joe White

Jeff Whitehead

Tom Whiting

Kevin Whitworth

Scott Whitworth

Bruce Williams

Kenny Williams

Tommy Williams

Kramer Williamson

Doug Wilson

Greg Wilson

Mark Wilson

Competitors in Heat Races, Consolation Features, and A Features at
Knoxville Raceway from 1990 to 2006 (Cont)

Tony Wilson
Kurt Winker
Kent Winters
Doug Wolfgang
Danny Wood
Mike Woodring
Cliff Woodward
Gary Wright
Lance Yonge
Ryan York
Danny Young
Jeff Young
Scott Young
Rick Ziehl
Dusty Zomer
Alan Zoutte

Spare Parts

In February of 1992, John, Brad, Smooth, and I got off the
porch and traveled to Florida to spectate at some Speed Week
sprint car races. The most unique was a couple of World of
Outlaws events held on a temporary track built inside the
Florida Suncoast Dome, now known as Tropicana Field.

On the first night we made our way through the pits, which
were located in the parking lot outside the dome, and wandered
in to take a look at the track. They called it a quarter-mile, but
it looked tiny and awfully flat. Future Hall of Fame announcer
Jack Miller happened to walk by as we were trying to figure out
what we were looking at.

Jack asked us, "What do you fellas think?"

We gave him a raised eyebrow, tilted-head, sucked-air-
through-teeth, "I'm not sure about this," response.

I do remember the races there were entertaining, but can't
for the life of me remember who won. I did extensive research
to find the results for those races (a couple of Google searches)
and found some fan records that said Steve Kinser won the
first night and Sammy Swindell won the second, which is
totally plausible for that era. I finally dragged out my old May
1992 issue of *Open Wheel Magazine* and was able to confirm.

Another interesting race we attended in Florida that year
was the first ever World of Outlaws/All Star Circuit of
Champions co-sanctioned pavement race at Charlotte County
Speedway in Punta Gorda. There was some discrepancy with

the "co-sanctioned" part. The Outlaws said it wasn't co-sanctioned because they ran under their rules, the All Stars said it was co-sanctioned, and the track just said dual points were awarded. Whatever it was, Dave Blaney won both races with the "limited pavement experience" he had at the time.

Jim Harris and I took a quick trip in October of 1991 and attended an All Star Circuit of Champions race at the tacky quarter-mile bullring in Bloomington, Indiana. We left on a Friday morning, made it to the race that evening, stayed at a hotel overnight, and came back home the next day. The trip made me appreciate the grueling schedule travelling race teams face, since they make that kind of journey regularly. Kevin Huntley won, followed by Jack Hewitt, and Danny Smith.

I have fond memories of the year-end gatherings the Twedts' hosted in Mike's garage in Huxley. They used these occasions as a way to say "thank you" to friends, family, and supporters, and never failed to provide a good time. I will also never forget the fish fries they threw in Knoxville, and that is the only place I ever ate the delicious "fish gravy" they concocted.

I've found it interesting to discover how drivers and teams come up with their car numbers. Some are handed down from generation to generation, others are random, and some have a certain meaning unknown to most.

Many are famous and immediately identifiable to sprint car fans: The #11 of Steve Kinser and the #1 of Sammy Swindell. The Weikert #29, Trostle #20, OFFIXCO #21x, and Sonner #47. The Bobby Allen #1a, Merrill #5m, and McCarl #7x. The Rogers #49, Schoff #23s, and Mickow #12. The Vielhauer #12x, Tuttle #10, and Robuck #12. The Hamilton #77, Hampshire #63, and Young #3Y. The Kreitz #69, ZEMCO #1, Apple #12, and Smith #19. The unusual like the Brickmobile #461, Hawkeye Stroebel #111, and Edd French #7777. Many more I'll remember later and regret not listing.

When Twedt started racing sprint cars he used Trostle's #20, then the #2 plus a "T" from his mini-sprint days. Jerry took the #12 from his motorcycle racing years, and added the "x" because the number was already in use by Lyle Sylvester.

The most entertaining number I remember was the #4Q used by Randi Turner. His t-shirts sported a picture of a fork next to a letter "U." The shirts also displayed a silhouette of a couple in the act of doing something normally completed behind closed doors. I wish I had purchased one of those shirts.

Indications that I may be a sprint car nerd:

I can't locate my racing t-shirt collection, and I'm sick about it. I'm missing my Wolfgang Weikert's #29, Knoxville 25th Anniversary, 1st Annual [sic] Limited Nationals, World of Outlaws Florida Suncoast Dome, World Wide Race Fans, Mike Twedt, and Jordan Albaugh shirts. And my Gaerte Race Engines hat. I had to have put them in a safe place.

I have been known to email DIRTvision when they haven't made a race available in the On Demand section in what I believe is a timely fashion.

I volunteered when DIRTvision asked for users to "beta test" in an effort to troubleshoot audio issues during live broadcasts. After listening to the two shows they asked us to track, I submitted spreadsheets which contained columns for time stamp, error code, and description of what I did to resolve problems. They replied and thanked me for my "detailed log" and said it was "very impressive."

I have listened to every single episode of the World of Outlaws official podcast, Open Red (including the trailer). And not just going back and binge listening, but when each episode originally aired.

In an early episode I received a shout-out when they asked where listeners were listening from, and I, of course, responded. Again during their "Crazy Race Fan Stories" episode, when I sent them the Danny Young helicopter story. And again when they had their Facebook Live mock World of Outlaws movie show, and I submitted Ed Harris to play Doug Wolfgang.

In 2002 my cousin and I made a trip to Ottumwa to purchase the Ratbag World of Outlaws PS2 sprint car video game. This is because the game was not to be found anywhere in the Des Moines area, I tracked one down in Ottumwa, and I wanted to obtain it "for my son for Christmas."

I'm not sure how much my son actually played it, but must admit that I have two careers going in the game. One has career earnings of $16,722,575 and balance of $15,824,665 in year 2025, and the other has career earnings of $67,927,825 and balance of $66,296,505 in year 2069.

It got to the point where I could regularly win every Outlaw feature in a season. If I didn't, it was usually due to getting taken out by cars flying unrealistically from inconceivable directions on those crazy tracks like Chico and I-55. I haven't played it for a few years, but when I turned it on to confirm the above numbers I kind of got the itch again. I may have a problem.

About

Jerry Crabb was born June 3, 1943. He raced motorcycles, 3-wheelers, and 4-wheelers from the 1960's into the 2010's. At the age of 47, in 1990 he made his first start in a 410 cubic inch sprint car at Knoxville Raceway. In 1991 he built his own 360 cubic inch sprint car and raced at Knoxville and several Iowa tracks until 2006. He was the winner of the 1998 Masters Classic at Knoxville Raceway. Jerry passed away on January 6, 2018.

Todd Thomas was a member of Jerry Crabb's pit crew from 1991 to 2006.

Printed in Great Britain
by Amazon

16690607R00119